OUR GOD REIGNS

For Dick & JoAnn –
Blessings on You always – As You
worship them!
Love
Phil

Our God Reigns: The Stories Behind Your Favorite Praise and Worship Songs

© 2000 by Phil Christensen and Shari MacDonald

Published by Kregel Publications, a division of Kregel, Inc., P.O. Box 2607, Grand Rapids, MI 49501. Kregel Publications provides trusted, biblical publications for Christian growth and service. For more information about Kregel Publications, visit our web site: www.kregel.com

Library of Congress Cataloging-in-Publication Data
Christensen, Phil and MacDonald Shari
   Our God reigns: the stories behind your favorite praise and worship songs / by Phil Christensen and Shari MacDonald
      p.   cm.
   1. Hymns, English—History and criticism.
I. MacDonald, Shari.   II. Title.
BV315.C47   2000   264'.23—dc21   00-030947
                                                        CIP
ISBN 0-8254-2369-4

Printed in the United States of America

1 2 3 4 5 / 04 03 02 01 00

OUR GOD REIGNS

The Stories Behind Your Favorite Praise and Worship Songs

PHIL CHRISTENSEN and
SHARI MACDONALD

kregel
PUBLICATIONS

Grand Rapids, MI 49501

Contents

PREFACE

For decades, churches have sung and clapped along with "He Has Made Me Glad."

I'll be candid. This dear little polka had grown a bit wearisome for me, especially as a worship leader. You might say that I was taking it for granted. But that all changed the day I spoke to Leona Von Brethorst and learned the story behind her sweet, simple song.

I discovered that years before, because of Leona's faith, her husband had abandoned her and her two small children. Bravely, Leona tackled life as a single mom, refusing welfare, working odd jobs, and raising her children to know the Lord. When her kids grew up and moved away, she found the "empty nest" almost too much to bear. Still, she clung to her determination to "enter His gates with thanksgiving" and trusted God to restore her joy. The Lord honored her commitment, and "He Has Made Me Glad" was born.

My knowing that story has made Leona's song more meaningful than ever to me, and my worship is sweeter because of it. As a worship pastor, I pray that as I've shared her words with my fellow saints, they, too, have found their worship to be enhanced and enriched.

Believers are told to "teach one another with . . . spiritual songs" (Colossians 3:16), and each of the stories you're about to read is brimming with truth—the sort often found deep in the trenches of the Christian battlefield. As Bob Fitts said, "I hope that writing good songs doesn't mean going through hard times, but I kind of think it does."

I suspect that Bob is right.

In these pages, you'll meet a schoolteacher who was fired repeatedly for leading his students to Christ. He found himself painting houses to support his family. His lesson to us? The song "Our God Reigns," a reminder that in God's sovereignty, Jesus' suffering and His glorification were not unrelated—and that our struggles, too, can bring honor and glory to Him.

You'll also read about a mother of two toddlers who lived in a small travel trailer in the desert while her husband attended Bible college. They were so poor that they had to choose between long-distance telephone calls home and milk. "I Love You, Lord" emerged from Laurie Klein's morning devotions during this time of sacrifice.

Similarly, most of these stories describe a moment when ordinary people encountered an extraordinary Lord, a Lord who left behind a song as a cherished souvenir of the rendezvous. In each story, the message and the messenger come together to weave a profoundly rich, deep tapestry of worship: a portrait of a mighty King who is also the Lover of our souls.

Each story here has been drawn from private interviews, and each composer—where possible—has personally reviewed the story to ensure the accuracy of both fact and tone. We want to thank these heroes of the faith for sharing their intimate stories.

Thanks also to Dennis Hillman and the other fine folks at Kregel Publications who have made this book a labor of love. They have been gracious and patient while I awkwardly juggled three hats—worship pastor, journalist, and husband/father. These friends have helped make the writing process a joy from the first telephone call to the final edit.

Special thanks to CCM Communications and *Worship Leader* magazine for their vision in publishing many of these articles over the years and for their kind permission to edit and reprint them here.

I'm so thankful that best-selling author, editor, and long-time friend Shari MacDonald agreed to join me on this project; her contributions have enhanced, more than I can express, the quality of the stories you're about to read. Her love for the English language and for God's people has brought polish and timelessness to these stories. I recommend her novels—and she's a pretty good piano player, too.

Thanks also to my friend, senior pastor Mike Whisner, and the dear congregation at the Church on the Mountain in the Hoodland Corridor of Oregon. Mike is the kind of supportive pastor that worship leaders pray for, and the kind of friend that I'm glad to have with me in the trenches of life and ministry.

Neither Mike nor the rest of my fellow worshipers at the Church on the Mountain have ever admitted to being weary of these stories, but have for years sweetly endured my lengthy song introductions. They've often said that understanding the hearts of these songwriters has enhanced their own worship. That's my prayer for you, too.

Credit must go where credit is due; God gave the idea for this book directly to my bride. That's not unusual, though, because the Lord has channeled nearly every *other* blessing in my life through Mitzi, too. There is no better homeschooling mom, no finer worship coleader, no more wonderful helpmate, and no Proverbs 31 woman that outshines her.

And she seldom complains that I tap away at my laptop computer in bed.

I would like to conclude this preface with a quotation from Audrey Mieir, author of "His Name Is Wonderful," who completed a follow-up interview with me just a few days before she went to be with the Lord:

"This song will outlive the chubby human hands chosen to write a few black notes on the five lines and four spaces. But it will never outlive the Father who glories in His Son's name and glories in our praise."

May these stories help you glory in His wonderful name.

—PHIL CHRISTENSEN

1

ALL HAIL, KING JESUS

DAVE MOODY

"I thought the song had flopped!"

For two thousand years, psalmists have savored the anticipation of King Jesus returning in all of His royal majesty. While a dozen stirring hymns have captured this anticipation, contemporary praise songs often lack the command—the almost military authority—that such a noble moment merits. A notable exception is Dave Moody's "All Hail, King Jesus."

"All Hail, King Jesus," with its simple, processional feel, is a royal welcome for Him who is enthroned upon our praises. The song addresses Jesus by five scriptural titles—King Jesus, Emmanuel, King of Kings, Lord of Lords, Bright Morning Star—layering them one upon another like multiple crowns. The chorus closes with a simple pledge to worship Him and reign with Him forever.

The musical life of its author, Dave Moody, was greatly shaped by Moody's older brother, Doug, under whom he studied piano. Eventually, Dave also assisted in his brother's music ministry duties at Glad Tidings Church in Vancouver, British Columbia, and joined him in teaching piano.

One Wednesday afternoon in January 1977, the younger Moody was playing the piano before he was to begin teaching. "I had some free time at home, so I went downstairs and began to play and just worship the Lord," he says. Crafting a timeless worship tune that would one day be sung all across the world was the thing furthest from Dave Moody's mind. "I had not intended to write a song and wasn't trying to manufacture anything; I simply wanted to spend time in the presence of the Lord." But as Moody played, something extraordinary began to unfold. "I suddenly realized that the Lord had given me a new song," he recalls. "It took only about five minutes for the song to come together, and it burned in my spirit for the rest of the week."

Moody, then twenty-eight years old, felt enthusiastic about the new anthem. "The theme of the song is the second coming of Christ. I could just imagine believers all over the world singing this song as Christ returned to earth," he says.

In fact, he was so excited, he decided to introduce it to his church the following Sunday. "The Lord gave me the opportunity to sing it during our morning service as I was playing the organ and leading worship." At the appropriate time in the service, Moody began to play and sing the piece, sure that the congregation would be moved by it. Without the benefit of an overhead or a slide, however, the song seemed to die somewhere between the microphone and the first row. "After singing the song through several times, I was about to stop, not sensing any response from the congregation.

"I remember being so disappointed," Moody recalls. "I thought the song had flopped!" Before he quit singing, however, his pastor encouraged him to lead the song once again. Moody complied. This time the response was quite different.

"I opened my eyes to see a congregation of about eight hundred people all on their knees, worshiping the Lord as they sang, 'All hail, King Jesus,'" Moody remembers. The worshipers were "bowing before the Lord, singing this chorus with all their strength! It was an incredible scene I shall never forget! We continued to worship the Lord for at least thirty to forty-five minutes longer," Moody says. God had used a newborn song powerfully to usher a congregation into the presence of His Son.

In the years since, Moody has made no effort to promote the piece. But the lips of worshipers have nevertheless carried it throughout the world. Reports have come back to him of "All Hail" being sung in Israel, Hungary, Russia, and countless other countries.

Although Moody has written twenty-five or thirty additional songs over the years, none of them has approached the broad appeal of his most widely recognized song.

"All Hail, King Jesus" became the title song of Integrity Music's third recording. The piece has since appeared in more songbooks, hymnals, recordings, arrangements, and musicals than its writer can remember. Moody himself went on to become a widely published songwriter and the music minister at Kent Christian Center in Kent, Washington. Yet, as far as the psalmist is concerned, the true story of the song's success is found not in achievements that can be seen, but in the hearts of worshipers who have used it as a tool to help them draw ever nearer to the Lord their God.

For now, Moody simply hopes that "All Hail" has helped people move beyond singing *about* Jesus into the realm of worshiping the Lord Himself. And he looks forward to the day when Christ shall return, and he can joyfully sing with countless other faithful believers. Here are the lyrics as originally written:

> *There is coming a day*
> *When time shall be no more*
> *And the clouds shall be rolled back as a scroll*
> *Then the Lord shall appear in all His glory*
> *With ten million saints singing love's sweet story . . .*
>
> *All hail, King Jesus!*
> *All hail, Emmanuel,*
> *King of Kings, Lord of Lords,*
> *Bright Morning Star.*
> *And throughout eternity,*
> *I'm going to praise Him,*
> *And forevermore*
> *I will reign with Him!*

"All Hail, King Jesus," Dave Moody, © 1981, Glory Alleluia Music. Lyrics reprinted by permission of the publisher.

2

As the Deer

MARTY NYSTROM

"I wasn't trying to write a chorus; I was just worshiping."

I t was not shaping up as a stellar summer.

Marty Nystrom had been determined to attend a summer session at Christ for the Nations Institute. The twenty-four-year-old school-teacher was looking forward to spending six weeks at the school in Dallas, Texas, and he was not going to be impeded by an airline strike. No planes? No problem. Nystrom bought a train ticket to Texas.

"I couldn't go directly to Dallas," he recalls. "I had to go through Chicago and then south. It was like three days of torture."

While it might appear to have been some noble spiritual quest, his sights were actually set on a young woman. Nystrom managed to finagle his way to the school during the summer of 1981. However, he soon learned that the relationship that he sought was not to be.

Nursing a bruised heart in strange surroundings left him bewildered. He couldn't help but notice that austere Christ for the Nations Institute lacked the manicured beauty of his old alma mater, Oral Roberts University. Worse yet, while he was at Oral Roberts University, Nystrom had acquired some crippling emotional baggage. "Although I had been involved in Christian ministry for some time, I could not say that my soul thirsted for more of God. I'd traded my initial desire to serve God in ministry for the need to win man's approval," he remembers.

At Christ for the Nations Institute, everything was adding up to a colossal zilch—and the sweltering Texas heat in July didn't help.

Why didn't he just go home? The answer was simple says Nystrom. "I didn't have a ticket."

A radical roommate convinced him that an extended fast would help him regain perspective. During the fast, Nystrom's sole source of refreshment came from the kitchen tap.

"It was just water," he remembers. "Dallas water."

Yet his soul, like a thirsty deer responding to a cool stream, began to respond to God. "Something about the fast immediately broke me," he explains. "God began to heal me of things that I didn't even know were there. I noticed that earthly desires and physical lusts began to wane. My spirit became more and more hungry for communion with God. For the first time in my Christian walk, I was able to pray Psalm 42:1 with sincerity."

Nineteen days into the twenty-one-day fast, Marty sat down to what he calls a "very out-of-tune piano" in the men's dorm and began spontaneously to sing out various psalms. He began to chord along to an old André Crouch song and worship the Lord quietly as he meditated on Psalm 42 of the King James Bible.

"God gave me a melody for Psalm 42:1. I just began to sing right off the page, literally," he recalls. "As far as I remember, I wrote the first section straight through."

"As the Deer" was born in those moments, and Marty repeatedly sang it to the Lord that day:

> *As the deer panteth for the water,*
> *So my soul longeth after Thee.*
> *You alone are my heart's desire,*
> *And I long to worship Thee. . . .*

The words came naturally.

"People ask me why I start off with King James and end up with contemporary language," says Nystrom. "I would never do that now; as a writer, I know better, but it was a spontaneous song, and I was reading out of the Bible. From there, I went off into my own response in my own language. I wasn't trying to write a chorus; I was just worshiping."

Friends encouraged him to share the song with worship leader Dave Butterbaugh at the school, and Nystrom sketched out a simple lead sheet. That framed manuscript now hangs in a hallway at Christ for the Nations Institute.

When "As the Deer" appeared on a school's worship tape in 1982, Nystrom was deluged with requests for permission to use the song. "I knew nothing about copyrights. I just had to write all these letters back, which I didn't enjoy," he remembers with a chuckle.

In 1983, Nystrom—who had become engaged to Jeannie, now his wife—returned to Christ for the Nations Institute to teach at the New York branch. It was a period when both campuses were seeing terrific praise music come to life; many students emerged as fine writers. Along with Nystrom, Sondra Corbett ("I Worship You Almighty God"), Tommy Walker ("Mourning into Dancing"), Eugene Greco ("Mighty Is Our God"), and others went on to become important contributors to Integrity Music and Maranatha! Music projects. "Probably twenty songs birthed at the school ended up being recorded by Integrity Music," Nystrom estimates.

After teaching at Christ for the Nations Institute for nearly five years, he joined the staff of Integrity Music where he worked as Song Development Manager for several years.

Since then, he has toured extensively with Worship International. "I've traveled to Asia twelve or thirteen times," he says. "They tell me that 'As the Deer' really rings true to the Asian heart, primarily melodically. It's very well received."

In every market tracked by Christian Copyright Licensing Incorporated (CCLI), "As the Deer" remains in the top twenty-five most licensed songs. In addition to "As the Deer," the composer has had eighty songs, many of them collaborations, recorded over the years. Of Integrity Music writers, Nystrom's works, along with those of Don Moen, appear most often in CCLI's top five hundred list. Nystrom has led worship on six Integrity Music projects.

"I marvel at all that," admits Nystrom. "I get excited when I go to a local church and I see one song after another on the overhead that I found or wrote or spoke to somebody about. But I could turn to anyone and tell them, and they couldn't care less!" he laughs. "I just thank God I was given the opportunity. Somebody else could have done the same thing."

Currently on staff at Eastside Foursquare in Bothell, Washington, Nystrom is enjoying the opportunity to draw the hearts of a younger generation to the living waters. "I think my experience with 'As the Deer' that summer was part of the preparation for me to do the kind of work I've done and stay—for the most part—free from the 'I did this' feeling," he says. "I know for a fact it was God who opened the doors."

Although "As the Deer" has made contemporary worship music history, Nystrom keeps his eyes on a single prize—the very one he had allowed to slip from his gaze during those days at Oral Roberts University. "I always go back to that summer when I could finally say, 'I want you, Jesus.' I know now the lack of satisfaction that comes from striving after man's approval. I've experienced that. I also know what it feels like to get the favor of God, and I know which I prefer."

"As the Deer," Martin Nystrom, © 1984, Maranatha! Music. Lyrics reprinted by permission of the author.

3

The Battle
Belongs to the Lord

JAMIE OWENS–COLLINS

"When we lift up the name of the Lord and we invite Him to rule in a situation, then He can come in and do His thing."

As the child of Jimmy Owens (whose song "Holy, Holy" has graced the pages of perhaps millions of hymnals) and Carol Owens (author of the equally popular Sunday morning favorite "Freely, Freely"), young Jamie Owens was born into a family where music was not only valued but also gratefully embraced as a means to shower the Lord with praises and lead God's children to His throne room.

Jamie first discovered a passion for music as she watched her parents worship, minister, and labor at their craft. Through God's grace, that passion would eventually birth a vision for music ministry that she would claim as her very own. By the mideighties, Jamie Owens-Collins (now married to music producer Dan Collins) had served in full-time music ministry for a dozen years and had traveled all across the world, leading worship and proclaiming the gospel through song.

During this time, she often reflected on the insights of Jack Hayford, under whose teachings she had long sat at the Church on the Way. From Hayford, Collins learned about the connection between spiritual warfare and praise and worship. She was impressed by the message of 2 Chronicles 20. In this passage, God promises the Israelites that He will deliver them from the armies of the Moabites, Ammonites, and Meunites and instructs them to go out to meet the enemy. The Israelites comply, appointing men to go out at the head of the army singing praises to the Lord.

"Obviously, there's no power in going out to sing just in itself," Collins acknowledges. "But they trusted in the Lord, and they obeyed Him. The Lord has put us in a position to invite His lordship into the earth. He won't just step in and do it very often. He waits for our invitation. When we lift up the name of the Lord and we invite Him to rule in a situation, then He can come in and do His thing."

Such truths were on Collins's mind one day as she prepared for a concert at Hope Chapel in Hermosa Beach, California. "I was in the car and just worshiping," she remembers. While she had in some cases spent years fine-tuning her songs, "The Battle Belongs to the Lord" was another matter entirely. "*Boom!*" she says. "It was just there. By the time I got to the church, I had it finished. I said, 'Hey, let's try this,' and taught it to everybody, and we sang it together *a cappella*."

"Buck Herring," of the Second Chapter of Acts, Collins notes, "calls those songs that you write in the car 'car tunes.'" This particular "car tune" of Collins's would spin its way onto her album *A Time for Courage*, released in 1985. The album, she says, "had to do with standing up and being a light in the world and knowing that we're stepping out into battle, but doing it anyway." Ironically, Jamie's own "time for courage" would soon be at hand.

Approximately five years after writing "The Battle Belongs to the Lord," Collins found herself locked in a debilitating four-year battle with clinical depression. "I had to walk through some real darkness. But even when I walked through the dark places, I still knew that the Lord hadn't changed, and that He was still worthy of my worship and of my praise. I couldn't sense the Lord at all," she says. But, like the musicians who marched into battle ahead of King Jehoshaphat's army, "I had to decide with my will that I was gonna trust Him."

"I had always considered myself a pretty strong person. I guess in a way, I finally saw myself for as weak as I really am. And that was a good thing. Because then the Lord pulled me out the other side of it, and I was able to see He was there all along."

At the time of her depression, Collins was shouldering multiple responsibilities, including those of music minister, songwriter, wife, and mother. "I had a huge amount on me at that time, to have three little kids and be traveling all the time and trying to write and record and everything. I had always liked that Scripture: 'I can do all things through Christ who strengthens me.' In my mind, I was thinking that meant I could do everything. I finally realized that what the Lord meant was that I needed to be sensitive and find out what He's given me to do. Because I can do everything *He's* given me to do, because He'll strengthen me to do it. But it doesn't mean I can do everything at once. He's unlimited, but we aren't."

Looking back, Collins views her extraordinary songwriting experience as a gift from God. She also sees the time she spent working at her craft as an invitation for God to work through her. "I've never been sort of awakened in the middle of the night. It just doesn't come completely out of the blue. But when I have been working on songs, and when I am singing to the Lord regularly, then every once in a while, here comes something!

"I think life is that way. There are times when God comes in and just, *boom!* answers your prayer right now and gives you a miracle. But, most of the time, He lets us really walk through the process. There seems to be something important to God about the process . . . just walking through one season after the next, letting each one do what it needs to so that fruit can finally be born."

The fruit that has come from God's blessings and Collins's labors can be seen easily. While "The Battle Belongs to the Lord" had what some people would view as a rocky start (one record label executive rejected it, telling Collins, "What you need is a *career builder*"), there is no question that today it is one of the most popular praise songs in circulation.

"The funny thing is, it's such a simple song," Collins marvels. "You know, I've written other songs that I feel were much more cleverly put together and crafted. This thing is just as simple as it can be, but that's the one. I don't know exactly how a song takes off.

"I guess in the end, you just have to say promotion comes from the Lord."

4

Blessed Be the Lord God Almighty

BOB FITTS

*"I hope that writing good songs
doesn't mean you have to go
through hard times, but . . .
I kind of think it does."*

From the opening line, Bob Fitts's "Blessed Be the Lord God Almighty" is brimming with passion and truth. In a mere sixteen measures, it tells as much about the character of God as it does the heart of a worshiper.

With pure and powerful lyrics layered over a flowing melody and chords that stair step heavenward, "Blessed Be" is effective, singable, and well written. That's what you'd expect, though, from a fellow like Bob Fitts.

Associated with Youth with a Mission since the early eighties, he founded the School of Worship at Youth with a Misson's University of the Nations in Kona, Hawaii, in 1990. In addition, he's done much worldwide to model excellence in worship.

Fitts has appeared as worship leader on a dozen fine worship recordings. He's in such demand as a teacher and worship leader that his schedule is jammed for a year in advance. Besides writing scores of great praise songs, he's also introduced the church to the finest writing of others through his recordings.

With peacock feathers like these in his cap, you might imagine that "Blessed Be the Lord God Almighty" was written between studio sessions while sipping guava nectar. Nothing could be further from the truth.

"I hope that writing good songs doesn't mean you have to go through hard times," he ponders, "but . . . I kind of think it does."

"Blessed Be" was, in fact, born of such hard times. In 1981, Fitts left a worship leading position in California to follow what he and his wife, Kathy, recognized as the prompting of the Lord. They packed a few belongings and took their infant and toddler to Kona to join Youth with a Mission.

In Kona, they found themselves involved in work quite different from what they had originally been told to expect. They felt disappointed and maybe even a little betrayed.

Their living conditions were, to say the least, "interesting," says Fitts. "They have houses over here called 'coffee shacks,'" he explains, laughing. "These are basically old buildings that were built for coffee farmers."

To put it simply, poverty in paradise with two small children was no luau for the Fittses. "I'd pretty much gotten to the end of my rope," he says.

One day, he was asked to sing and play a special number at a local church. Fitts accepted the offer, but his confidence and creativity were at low ebb. He couldn't even think of a song to play.

"I was discouraged," he says, remembering how he thought: "Maybe I'll just write a song." Picking up his guitar, he began to touch the strings and sing. "Blessed Be the Lord God Almighty" was born on the spot. "The song just came," says Fitts. "Really in five or ten minutes." He sensed the hand of God in the song and decided to play it for the church the following morning.

Unfortunately, the song slipped from his mind. Worse, he had failed to record it.

"So I got up in front of this church, trying to sing it, and basically faked it the whole way through," he says, chuckling as he recalls the incident.

The song, though, would not be silenced. "On the way home from church, it came back to me," Fitts explains. "I went home and put it on a cassette."

From there, Youth with a Mission worship teams began to take it all over the world. At the same time, Fitts was invited to join a tour with David and Dale Garrett of Scripture in Song, which increased the song's exposure.

It was first recorded in 1984 on Fitts's own *Take My Healing to the Nations*, but it has since appeared on Maranatha! Music and Integrity Music projects. Since then, he says, "I can go just about anywhere in the world and people will recognize it."

Perhaps the most memorable experience came when Fitts was standing in Seoul, Korea, as thousands began singing "Blessed Be" in Korean. As he watched the Jumbotron® pan the huge crowd of worshiping Asian faces, he was overwhelmed. "It was too much for me," he recalls fondly. "I just started crying!"

Much has changed in his life since the time he sang the song in a coffee shack. His family has grown from two to four children. The Fittses no longer live in poverty. And his personal dream to exalt Jesus in the nations has come to pass not only in his life but also in the life of his family. "I just got off the phone with my oldest boy, Andy, who was one year old at the time of the writing of the song," Fitts said not long ago. "He's now in Europe traveling with a praise band."

Fitts is no longer directing the School of Worship, but he remains based in Kona where his work still operates under Youth with a Mission. And Fitts still clearly remembers exactly who brought him through that time of discouragement during his early days in Kona. "There is no failure in our lives, no height of success that is greater than the God we serve. He is above all and worthy of praise in both circumstances. Both when He has you in a coffee shack in Hawaii wondering why you're stuck on a rock out in the middle of the Pacific Ocean or when you're standing in a stadium with close to one hundred thousand people from a different nation using a song that you wrote in that little coffee shack.

"At those two extremes, and everything in between, God is awesome, awesome, awesome. He never changes; He's always good. Music is just a tool to say that."

5

Everything's Gonna Be Alright in Christ

DENNIS POLEN

*His songwriting partners were
embarrassed that he wanted to
include it with the demo tape. . . .
After all, this cassette was a
professional production.*

I
t was almost a nursery rhyme," Denny Polen admits. Put off by
the simplicity of "Everything's Gonna Be Alright in Christ," his
songwriting partners were embarrassed that he wanted to include it
with the demo tape they were sending to Maranatha! Music.

Having recently left the fold of the Church On the Way to become a worship leader at a Foursquare church in the San Fernando
Valley, Denny Polen had thrown himself into one of the most enjoyable tasks related to his new position: writing songs to be performed on Sunday mornings as specials during tithes and offerings.

In addition to his role as worship leader, Polen was working a
day job during weekdays and writing scores for network TV shows
with his songwriting partners. Recently, the team had begun to write
Christian tunes and record elaborate demo tapes to send out to
Christian labels. When Polen suggested including one of the first
songs he had written as his church's worship leader, his partners
balked. After all, this cassette was a professional production, packed
with well-crafted songs.

And so, over his partners' objections, Polen secretly added a poor
recording of "Everything's Gonna Be Alright in Christ."

"I sort of snuck it in as the last song," he confesses, explaining, "I always just knew that the Lord wanted to use that song."

Polen was right.

Despite being presented via what Polen calls "the least of all" demo recordings, the song was an immediate hit with the folks at Maranatha! Music. It has since appeared on numerous Maranatha! Music recordings, including the classic *Live Worship with Bob Fitts and the Maranatha! Singers*. Praise Band covered the piece in *You're So Faithful*. It has also appeared in both *A Capella Praise* and the *Kids Praise* series. The group Nothing to Dread released a reggae version on Star Song records.

The simple piece is a musical paraphrase of Romans 8:28, born in a time of trial and struggle. "I wrote it to sing [with] our congregation, but I really wrote it to minister to me," says Polen. In 1988, the multitude of tasks related to worship leading, single fatherhood, writing, and other roles were taking a toll on Polen's spirit. "I was going through a major wilderness experience," he says, "having a hard time balancing all these responsibilities and duties. I was struggling with some health issues, but God kept telling me to be anxious for nothing."

In the midst of this storm, the song arrived with a very gentle, legato feel. What is sung today as the second verse actually came to him first.

> *When your troubles leave you numb,*
> *Everything's gonna be alright in Christ.*
> *By His blood you will overcome,*
> *Everything's gonna be alright in Christ.*
> *Lift your hands and praise His name,*
> *For eternity the same;*
> *His mercies we proclaim,*
> *Everything's gonna be alright in Christ.*

The rest of the song followed, and Polen added the familiar breezy rhythm.

"I recorded it on a tape and presented it to the church a week later, in its incredible simplicity." Polen says he didn't have a great deal of faith in the piece until he realized how his congregation was responding. It immediately became a favorite there and was sung often. "I knew when I did it in church it ministered to people," he recalls.

As he saw God's restorative touch "eye to eye," his loyalty to the piece grew.

"I just really had some good feelings about it. And when Maranatha! Music called up, I remember being really happy." Polen says he laughed, slapped his knee, and thanked the Lord for taking glory in "the least of all."

Describing the source of the song, Polen assumes little credit for it. "It's interesting to see what the Lord does. Sometimes He takes the least obviously interesting [song] and takes it and exalts it to where He wants to put it."

Polen voices his view that songwriting is a gift. "The Lord is the giver of these gifts. I would seem ludicrous to think it could be any other way. Never in my life did I doubt that it was the Lord. Even before I came to the Lord, I always knew the ability to write songs did not come from me." Polen explains that many times he "hears" new songs in his head, in their entirety—complete with words, music, arrangement, and accompaniment. Such was the case with "Everything's Gonna Be Alright in Christ." "That one was just there one day," Polen explains.

Although time has passed since Polen's humble song first sky-rocketed to popularity, this beloved tune remains dear to his heart. "I praise God for the way that song has ministered to people, but [it] has ministered to me more than anybody else. God just constantly encourages and reminds me. When you're walking in obedience to the Lord, doing your best for Him, and you have a heart for Him in everything that you do, it may not [always] look like you're out of the wilderness. It may not look like circumstances around you are being worked out by the Lord."

At such times, Polen cautions, believers should resist all temptation to give in to doubt. "Fear creeps up on even the most heartfelt believers. Songs such as this really minister to people when they even embrace a doubt at all. The Lord said, and you will say to this mountain, be moved and if you do not doubt it in your heart, it will. Doubt is our worst enemy, and doubt is where the Devil uses all of his tricks. The second we doubt in our heart, even if we don't speak it, we immediately begin to erode our own confidence in what the Lord has already done. [But] He has already done all these things for us. By His stripes we were healed."

A decade after it was written, Polen's most well-known song is affecting more lives than ever before. Denny tells the story of walking into a Bible study recently. New friends were singing "Everything's Gonna Be Alright in Christ," unaware that he was the author. "It's really cool to see your tunes come back at you through people in local assemblies of worship," he muses. "Nothing blesses me more."

Permission secured from Maranatha! Music for use of the lyrics from "Everything's Gonna Be Alright in Christ" (Maranatha! Music, © 1989).

6

GIVE THANKS

HENRY SMITH

*"It was just another song at the time.
It didn't stand out as being special;
it was just better than average."*

Deep in the heart of inland China, six Youth with a Mission missionaries were facing failure. This small team had committed to a grueling prayer-walk, seeking members of China's besieged underground church. They were looking for Chinese Christians. It was hardly an easy task. Such persecuted believers had learned long ago not to reveal themselves to strangers. On a boat trip far up the Yellow River, the team found a small village with a dark, dirty cafe where they rested and ate. Acting on a prompt from within his heart, one team member began to quietly hum Marty Nystrom's "As the Deer." Joy rushed through the hearts of the young missionaries as they recognized what they were hearing from a distant booth. A sweet voice was humming—in response—the haunting melody of Henry Smith's "Give Thanks."

The exchange of melodies gave the cautious Chinese a sense of safety, and they gladly embraced their new Western friends. The Youth with a Mission team discovered that many believers were in the area, and they returned home with a fresh understanding of the Chinese church.

That story encouraged Henry Smith with a sense of just how global his little song has become. "Give Thanks" has traveled to places that he is unlikely to visit. The composer is legally blind and hasn't even driven a car since 1981.

Skillfully built from a bucketful of chords and a playful melody, "Give Thanks" resonates with raw emotion. It focuses our hearts on the infinite goodness of God and the joy of pouring out our appreciation to Him. Even after many years, the powerful chorus is no less majestic.

> *And now let the weak say, "I am strong!"*
> *Let the poor say, "I am rich*
> *Because of what the Lord has done for us!"*
> *Give thanks.*

Smith wrote the song in 1978, shortly after graduating from Union Theological Seminary in Richmond, Virginia. Seminary had been pretty rough for the soft-spoken North Carolina boy. A degenerative eye disease had made it difficult to keep up with his heavy reading load. In addition, he'd found academia very dry and denominationalism extremely disappointing.

With joy, he pocketed his sheepskin and moved to be near his home church in Williamsburg. He returned to that Pentecostal ministry as a layman and worked odd jobs to support himself. "This was not a good career move for a guy who had just graduated from a Presbyterian seminary," Smith remembers, "but I saw God moving there."

He also saw there a young woman named Cindy Blanchard, and the two were soon engaged. Although Smith was struggling with his eyesight and having difficulty finding long-term employment, he was thrilled to be out of school, to be worshiping with friends in a vibrant church, and to be in love.

"I remember being extremely thankful," says Smith of those days, "and I remember my pastor quoting 2 Corinthians 8:9, that Christ, though He was rich, became poor for our sakes that we might become rich in Him."

And, as he had often done over the years, he wrote a song about it.

Give thanks with a grateful heart,
Give thanks to the Holy One,
Give thanks because He's given Jesus Christ, His Son.

"It was just another song at the time," Smith explains. "It didn't stand out as being special; it was just better than average."

However, this little "better than average" praise piece soon began a mysterious journey that may never be fully understood.

In 1986, "Give Thanks" emerged as the title song—and the crown jewel—of Integrity Music's seventh recording. Early copies of that project listed the author as unknown while Integrity Music continued to search for the composer. Somehow, the song's trail led through Switzerland, but Integrity Music then hit a dead end. Eventually, a friend of Smith's heard the recording and Smith contacted the publisher to inform them of the song's authorship.

"There's no room for boasting on my part, because God really did it," says Smith. "Someone in my church asked me how to make a song a 'hit' so a lot of people would hear it. I told her I didn't know how to do that because I didn't do it before! God moved it all over the place while we were right here in Virginia."

Today Smith runs a recording studio while his wife operates a small business, but the royalties from "Give Thanks" have supplemented their income for many years, freeing them to be available for ministry. Still active in music, Smith plays bass for the local worship team and works with the youth ministry. When leading worship with guitar or keyboard, the songwriter depends on his memory instead of his eyesight; he doesn't have the option of glancing down at an upcoming chord or lyric.

Of the disability, Smith says, "It slows me down, but it doesn't stop me!"

His zeal for God, however, cannot be diminished. Smith encourages worship leaders not to be distracted by the demands for flash and showmanship. "Be primarily a worshiper of God," he says, "and please Him first; don't get caught up in the fear of man or the man-pleasing trap."

Smith's wife, Cindy, says, "Henry's written many songs, but I think this one ministers to the heart of the Father. Any daddy wants his kids to say, 'thanks,'" she says, "to be recognized."

Could this be the reason behind the song's popularity? Smith does not even hazard a guess. "The only explanation I have," he says, "is that God is sovereign. He does what He does."

7

HE HAS MADE ME GLAD

LEONA VON BRETHORST

"I don't know a note of music or how to play any instrument!"

When I first heard "He Has Made Me Glad," I was a busboy pouring coffee for an aging Women's Aglow group. A little blue-haired pianist pumped out a polka beat while those old saints clapped like school girls on each syllable of the chorus.

I wasn't yet a believer, but I knew these women; some of them had been widowed or abandoned, others were riddled with cancer, some were raising their grandchildren. My heart was moved as brittle, battle-worn voices rang with supernatural joy:

> *He has made me glad, He has made me glad;*
> *I will rejoice for He has made me glad.*

Although Leona Von Brethorst's classic praise song overflows with triumph, the composer didn't have many obvious reasons to be glad.

Born in 1923 in the Smoky Mountains of East Tennessee, Leona was raised in abject poverty. "We didn't know we were poor," she says, because "everyone else was like us." She remembers going to school without shoes while she and her sister shared three dresses. She and her ten siblings also shared the arm's-length attention of a harsh father.

Her mother, though, was a devout believer who handled medical emergencies with prayer and home medicine since the nearest doctor was many miles away. "There were a lot of times we could have died," Leona remembers, "but my mother prayed us through."

Cold winters kept them home for a portion of the year, but in the summer the family walked three miles to a Full Gospel church. The heart-felt praise of Appalachian saints made a deep impression on the young woman. Fiddles, guitars, and banjos rang through the valley while some clogged before the Lord. "It was tremendous!" Von Brethorst recalls. "They'd really get happy and dance!"

"I always had a real desire in my heart for the things of God," she says of those early years. Von Brethorst remembers praying to have the same kind of meaningful encounters with God that others in the church seemed to know. That quest lead her to a literal mountaintop experience as a child. Craving a deeper encounter with God, she hiked to the peak of a local mountain, where she supposed she might be closer to Him. As she prayed, she looked out. "The whole valley was filled with people! I knew that if I talked, they would hear me."

Von Brethorst's childhood faith faded during World War II as she took a job in the defense plants in Detroit. After the war, she married and had her two children.

When her toddler became critically ill with polio-related seizures, she cried out in faith, begging, "If You don't let him die, I'll give the rest of my life to You." God did heal the child, and doctors confirmed the miracle.

The joy of her renewed faith was overshadowed by her husband's distaste for Christianity. He laid down an ultimatum: choose between him and Jesus.

Leona chose Jesus.

She never remarried. "Bob was the only man I ever loved," she says simply, yet she never regretted giving her whole heart to the Lord. As a single mom, she battled exhaustion and clinical depression. She worked odd jobs that brought her home before her children returned from school, focused all of her efforts on being a good mom to her kids, and devoted herself to making sure her children knew the Lord. During those years, she discovered her gifts as a worship leader. She wrote dozens of praise songs and taught them to her fellowship. "God would give me the melody to every word," she explained. "I don't know a note of music or how to play any instrument!"

"He Has Made Me Glad" sprang not out of the abandonment, poverty, and depression she had experienced but out of the silence of an empty nest— the devastating loneliness that came from seeing her children grown and moved away. The song was God's way of teaching her that thanksgiving is the key to experiencing the joy of the Lord. "He Has Made Me Glad" followed spontaneously.

The morning she taught the song to Calvary Fellowship, Von Brethorst says laughter and dancing erupted and lasted for hours. The youth of the church soon took it with them to a summer camp, where it began its global journey.

Now found in every modern hymnal and songbook—for many years among the top five most licensed praise songs through Christian Copyright Licensing Incorporated—"He Has Made Me Glad" has both brought joy to believers worldwide and provided income for Von Brethorst, allowing her needs to be met yet again by God's blessing. (A comedy of copyright blunders resulted in the song's being attributed to Mel Ray, author of "Arise and Sing," but this error was corrected and Leona's retirement was eventually funded by the royalties from her song.)

Pondering the song's enduring popularity, Von Brethorst exclaims, "It's strange! I don't feel different than anyone else singing it. I do feel the Lord has blessed the song because it contains the Bible's pattern for worship. We *do* enter His gates with thanksgiving, and His courts with praise," she adds. "It's a choice we make."

"I believe worship leaders are as important as senior pastors; you can cause the Word of God to lodge in people's hearts through worship." The secret, she says, is "to stay very close to the Holy Spirit"—the same Spirit who once gave her the vision of the multitude to whom she would one day minister. Looking back now to the mountaintop experience of her childhood, Von Brethorst admits, "I just forgot it [at the time]." Now, however, she compares it to the dreams of Joseph, saying, "This song has gone to the nations."

8

His Name Is Wonderful

AUDREY MIEIR

"I did not know at that strangely moving moment that a once-in-a-lifetime experience was about to happen."

Why is it so easy to love the classic praise song that begins "His name is wonderful . . ."?

Is it those four descending piano notes? The familiar phrases that stair-step with authority? That ever-surprising B♭? It could be all of these factors; the piece is well-crafted.

Beyond this, though, there is an intangible sense of "rightness" here. When we hear this song, the throne room doesn't seem very far away.

Audrey Mieir's simple "His Name is Wonderful" has won a permanent place in our hearts. It has remained a favorite through decades of stylistic and cultural turbulence.

From where did it come? Surprisingly, this is a Christmas composition. And the story behind it is nearly as remarkable as the song itself.

In 1955, Christmas fell on a Sunday. That day, at Bethel Union Church in Duarte, California, young and old alike shared a homespun church Christmas program. Audrey's brother-in-law, Luther, was the pastor.

Little shepherds dressed in bathrobes quietly clutched canes that passed for staffs. A teenage Mary cradled a plastic doll. A grinning angel with a crooked halo waved at Mom and Dad in the second row.

The choir, having sung about sleeping in "heavenly peace," sat down in reverent silence. Then the pastor stood to address the little congregation, his heart brimming with the beauty of Isaiah 9:6:

"For unto us a child is born, unto us a son is given; and the government will be on His shoulder; and His name shall be called Wonderful, Counselor, the Mighty God, the Everlasting Father, the Prince of Peace."

With eyes closed and hands raised, he broke the hushed silence and simply said, "His name is wonderful."

"I did not know at that strangely moving moment," Audrey Mieir recalled, "that a once-in-a-lifetime experience was about to happen." She described hearing a rustling sound, like that of angels' wings, followed by a beautiful new chorus. She scribbled it into the flyleaf of her Bible as quickly as her pen could release its ink:

> *His name is Wonderful,*
> *His name is Wonderful,*
> *His name is Wonderful,*
> *Jesus, my Lord.*
>
> *He is the mighty King,*
> *Master of everything,*
> *His name is Wonderful,*
> *Jesus, my Lord.*

Having written scores of songs before and since, Audrey Mieir does not recall a piece ever making its entry quite like this. She taught it to young people that night while it was still only a chorus. Later—over a burger, a cola, and a concordance—she completed the bridge:

> *He's the Great Shepherd,*
> *The Rock of all ages,*
> *Almighty God is He.*
>
> *Bow down before Him,*
> *Love and adore Him,*

His name is Wonderful,
Jesus, my Lord.

Since then, the song has been translated into every major dialect. Mieir heard it being sung in four different languages at the Vatican in the presence of the Pope. She fondly recalled hearing it sung in the Garden of Gethsemane. It is sung in Taiwan, in Sweden, and throughout Korea and the Philippines. The author once heard thousands of students in Hong Kong sing it from their rooftop schools.

At Explo '72, a Christian young people's convention in Dallas, Texas, a torrential downpour and thunderstorm ended one evening's festivities at the Cotton Bowl. Before leaving the stadium, the rainsoaked crowd of seventy thousand spontaneously lifted "His Name Is Wonderful" far above the storm and earthshaking thunder.

Remembering the birth of the piece, she said, "I did not foresee the ministry one little song of praise could have."

Recounting one of her favorite stories about the song, she reflected upon the time she was approached by a stranger at a bookseller's convention, where Mieir was making an appearance. "I saw a little old lady leaning against the wall, watching me," Mieir said. "When she saw me, she came as fast she could over to the piano and said, 'Audrey. I've just got to tell you this. My husband and I sang together for years. He had a beautiful tenor voice. We were always a favorite duet team.'"

One day the couple was together when they overheard someone singing the familiar "His Name Is Wonderful." The man turned to his wife and said, "Darling, this is my favorite song that's ever been written. Don't ever forget."

Only a few weeks later, the woman was called to the hospital where she found her husband in bed, dying. "He looked up at me," she told Mieir, "and he said, 'Mother, let's sing it one more time. Our favorite song.'"

"Audrey," the woman said, "we sang it, and his voice was beautiful like it used to be." Then, "all of a sudden, he died . . . singing your song." And so the man entered into Jesus' presence, singing:

His name is Wonderful,
His name is Wonderful,
His name is Wonderful,
Jesus, my Lord.

Mieir often shared this story as an illustration and testimony of the fact "that God knows what we need when we need it. After I put my arms around that little lady and prayed for her, she left," Mieir said. "I never saw her again. But I knew I'd meet her in heaven someday."

On November 5, 1996, Audrey Mieir, too, went to be with her Lord. Before she died, the veteran worshiper said of "His Name Is Wonderful," "The song will outlive the chubby human hands chosen to write a few black notes on the five lines and four spaces. [But it] will never outlive the Father who glories in His Son's name and glories in our praise."

"His name is full of awe. It is truly wonderful."

And now, at long last, she's telling Him so face-to-face.

"His Name Is Wonderful," Audrey Mieir, © 1959, Manna Music. Lyrics reprinted by permission of the author.

9

HOLY GROUND

GERON DAVIS

"When [we] come into God's presence, we're all on level ground. And it's holy ground."

Some songs seem to *insist* upon being born. And nothing—not even teenage overconfidence and procrastination—can get in their way. Perhaps no one knows this better than Geron Davis.

In 1979, nineteen-year-old Davis was helping to prepare the new building that his church congregation, pastored by his father, would soon call home.

"We had just completed a brand new sanctuary in the little town of Savannah, Tennessee," he says. "About six weeks before we moved into the new place, my dad started saying, 'Son, I wish you'd write us a new song for the first Sunday service.'"

Davis, who had been writing songs since his earliest teenage years, replied, "Okay, Dad. I'll do it."

After a couple of weeks, Davis's father asked, "Son, you got that song?"

He replied, "No, Dad, but I'll do it."

A similar exchange followed weeks later.

"How about it, man? You got that song for us?"

"No, Dad, but you know me, and I'll write the song."

On the Saturday before the new building's dedication, church members worked all day preparing for the opening service. At midnight, after the other laborers had left, Davis's father turned to him once again and asked, "Son, did you get us a special song for the first service?"

Davis answered, "No, sir. But I'm fixin' to!"

Once his father had left, Geron finally sat down at the church's shiny new grand piano and thought, *What do we want to say when we come into this place for the first time?*

The answer came without hesitation.

"Literally, as fast as I could write the words down," Davis says, "they were there. Within about ten or fifteen minutes, I had the entire song finished."

As I walked through the door, I sensed His presence,
And I knew this was a place where love abounds.
For this is a temple, Jehovah God abides here.
We are standing in His presence, on holy ground.

Did Davis realize that he had written something powerful?

"Are you kidding?" he laughs. "I was a nineteen-year-old kid, dead-tired on my feet. I was ready to go get into bed!"

The next morning, Davis shared the song with his sister and brother. "I taught them the parts, and we sang it in church. The power of God moved in. . . . It was a wonderful time. Of course, my mother was in the audience, so I expected everybody to love the song! But, you know, I didn't really understand at that point what God had done."

Soon thereafter, Davis helped record "Holy Ground" for a friend's album. Another friend heard the recording and asked permission to shop the song around. Twenty-four hours later, she returned to Davis with news that Meadowgreen Music was interested.

When the company signed "Holy Ground," music executive Randy Cox told Davis, "This song will live beyond you. It will be bigger than you can imagine."

Yeah, yeah. Sure, sure, Davis remembers thinking. "But you know what? He was on target."

Although the song was not recorded by any major vocal artists at that time, it quickly caught on in the church and in 1986 was distinguished as Word Music's best-selling anthem; by the end of the millennium, it remained Word's second-best-selling anthem of all time. It has been recorded by countless artists and has appeared in more than a half-dozen hymnals.

Davis speculates that the reason for the song's popularity lies in its accessibility.

"The most satisfying thing is not how many units we've sold or how much money it's made, but the fact that I have done something that becomes a part of the fabric of people's everyday lives," he says. "It's not just something they sing on Sunday, but something they sing in the special moments of their lives: at weddings, at funerals, in times of sickness, in times of trouble, in times of heartache.

"It blows me away that God will take a little country boy from the foothills of Tennessee and let him write a song as a teenager that would have the effect and the impact that this one's had. It just kind of proves that little is much when God is in it."

In addition to touching the hearts of the "average" man and woman, "Holy Ground" has also spoken into the lives of the rich and famous. While still serving as the governor of Arkansas, Bill Clinton became a fan of the song. Following his election to the presidency, Clinton invited Davis and his wife, Becky, along with their choir, to sing "Holy Ground" at his inauguration, in the presence of such celebrities as Colin Powell, Alec Baldwin, and Kim Basinger. When Bill Clinton's mother, Virginia Kelley, died in 1994, the president asked that "Holy Ground" be sung at her funeral. It was at Kelley's memorial that her good friend Barbra Streisand first heard the song. Streisand later wrote in the liner notes for her album *Higher Ground,*

> It's hard for me to describe that electrifying moment. The music united us . . . elevating our spirits with every note. I knew then that I had to sing that song, and others like it. The idea for this album was born at that moment. . . .

The lyrics say that whenever we stand in the presence of God, we're on holy ground. But since God is all around us, that would make every inch of this beautiful planet holy ground.

After the album's release, someone asked Geron Davis, "How does it feel to know that you 'electrified' Barbra Streisand?"

Davis replied, "Give me a break. I mean, I was born in the night, but it wasn't *last* night. Here's a lady who's sung on Broadway. She has sung duets with every famous person in the country. She's produced, starred in, and directed movies. She holds the Guinness title for the most multiplatinum female artist in American music. You name it, she's done it. And you think a nineteen-year-old's song is gonna electrify her? That's not what electrified Barbra Streisand. What happened to Barbra Streisand—and I believe she would agree—is that she got into the presence of the King of Kings and the Lord of Lords. She was electrified, not by my song, not by the singer, but by the presence of God that she felt in the room.

"The presence of God has the same effect on everybody. It doesn't matter how powerful, how big, how popular, how wealthy, how well known you are. When [we] come into God's presence, friend, we're *all* on level ground. And it's *holy* ground."

"Holy Ground," Geron Davis, © 1983, Meadowgreen Music Company. Lyrics reprinted by permission of the author.

10

I LOVE TO LOVE YOU

KIM BOLLINGER

"On the way to the retreat, I was praying, really pleading with God, 'Please give me a song!'"

When worship leaders sort through their favorite praise ballads, Kim Bollinger's "I Love to Love You" often hovers at the top of their lists. The song first appeared on Kent Henry's 1993 *Secret Place* Integrity Music recording, and has since found a home in hearts around the world.

With imagery that includes beholding God through an opened veil, the song borrows freely from a half-dozen Scripture passages, which are skillfully woven together to express—really, explain—the wonder of worship. Awestriking solo verses give way to a sweet congregational chorus.

A Missouri native, Kim was born and raised in rural Fredericktown. Her family was musical and involved in their local church. "I've loved the Lord as far back as I can remember," she says. "I always wanted to serve God. From the time I was eight or nine years old, I wanted my life to be set apart for Him."

She began to write songs at about the same age. In a small country church, these songs easily found their way into the congregation's worship. "I won't brag on the songs, but they served the purpose of the people and the place," she recalls.

Kim's childhood passion was for God; her heroes were radical Christians. "I used to admire Brother Andrew and other missionaries who smuggled Bibles. That's what I wanted to do."

As she grew up, she found her desire for deeper intimacy with God bumping against the denominational boundaries of her church. "They had some funny theologies that I just couldn't buy. I loved so many of the people, but I was looking for more of a personal encounter with the Holy Spirit. Still, I stayed with it until I went to college."

Her "Christian" college experience was even more frustrating, since she encountered very little spiritual focus. "But it was where I had my scholarship," she explains. "I just dug my heels in and stayed. I was really kind of a loner, dedicated to the Lord." During those years, she led Bible studies and kept writing songs. "I made the best of it," she says.

Kim married Scott Bollinger, and they joined a church that eventually became Victory Fellowship in St. Louis. Kim filled the worship leader's vacancy left by Kent Henry. During this period, she wrote "I Love to Love You." She tells the story.

"Around 1990 or 1991, we were doing a women's retreat. My job was to lead worship and also to speak. The subject of the retreat was worship, and my teaching was from Hebrews chapter ten. I was preparing a talk about how the veil was rent and how the blood of Jesus not only paid for our sins and gave us an eternal hope, but how it also gave us access to the throne room of the Father.

"I'd been asked to write a theme song for the retreat, and for two months, I had been praying that God would give me a song. But nothing was coming, and I was feeling pretty bad about it. I had come up with alternatives. On the way to the retreat, I was praying, really pleading with God, 'Please give me a song!' I unpacked, and twenty minutes before the meeting where I was supposed to speak, I went into the sanctuary. It's right on a lake, a big glass window in the back, a beautiful place. I just sat and worshiped the Lord. I felt like God said, 'You're just striving; you've got this all prepared—quit worrying about it, and spend some time with Me.'

"So I did. And right at that moment . . ." Kim strikes the palms of her hands together, "the entire chorus of the song just started to flow out of me as I played. I sang it as the words and music happened spontaneously. Then the verses began to come. I jotted them down real quick. This all happened within ten or fifteen minutes."

Only moments later, women at the retreat were singing "I Love to Love You," reading the lyrics from a handwritten overhead transparency. As she taught the new piece, Kim battled a nagging fear that she might forget the music at any moment, but she didn't.

"We sang the song during the retreat, over and over. It was the instrument the Lord used to do much ministry that weekend. We introduced it to the church when we got back home, and they began to use it, too."

Kent Henry was fond of the song and taught it at his praise events; he eventually included "I Love to Love You" and Kim's "Spirit, Touch Your Church" on his 1993 Integrity Music project.

The song has since gone around the world. "When I was a little girl, I prayed to be a missionary," Kim recalls, "but was never really able to go." As letters of appreciation came from places as distant as Mongolia, a beautiful realization came to her. "It dawned on me that God had been able to use me as a missionary through this recording!"

Beyond that, the song has opened the door for Kim to serve cross-culturally in places like Singapore, Malaysia, Indonesia, and throughout the United States. "It touches me that God would cause this music to go before me so that people would embrace me, even though they didn't know me."

Kim, her husband Scott, and their three daughters live in St. Louis, Missouri, where Kim serves as Music Director at Bethesda Evangelical Church.

When asked if she has a word for worship leaders, she says, "Stay married to the original promptings of the Lord in your work, whether you're writing songs or leading worship or whatever. Stay in intimate contact with your Source and your Resource, which is Jesus. It's so easy to get distracted and down the wrong path, there's so much glitter and glamour offered. Stay faithful to the original calling the Lord put in your heart."

11

I Love You, Lord

LAURIE KLEIN

"I feel like God not only gave me the song, but He kissed it."

A remote mobile home gleams faintly in the crisp autumn sunrise. Within that metal refuge in the high desert of Central Oregon, a young mother is having a quiet time with the Lord. Her toddler is still asleep. Her husband is a full-time college student, and the couple is surviving on $400 per month. They have no home church and no friends nearby, and she does not drive. Even the expense of a long-distance telephone call might leave them without milk or bread in weeks to come.

Such is the backdrop of Laurie Klein's classic praise song, "I Love You, Lord," written in 1974.

"It was a very hopeless time, a very depressed time," she summarizes. "I felt the poverty of my own life keenly at that point, both emotionally and physically." Klein cites Hosea 2:14, in which the Lord says, "I will lead her into the desert and speak tenderly to her," saying that that's exactly what happened in her own life.

"That morning I was so empty," she says, recalling her time with the Lord. "I knew I didn't have anything to offer Him. And so I asked if He would like to hear me sing . . . if He would just give me something He would be in the mood to hear."

Laurie describes "I Love You, Lord" as a gift from God that emerged spontaneously from her lips. "The song came like an early Valentine. It just leaped into my mouth. I sang the first half and put the chords with it with no effort," she says.

I love You, Lord, and I lift my voice
To worship You, O my soul rejoice.

Intrigued and moved by these words, she remembers thinking, *Maybe I should write that down.* She stopped long enough to get a pen; when she came back, the last two phrases came just as easily.

Take joy, my King, in what you hear,
May it be a sweet, sweet sound in Your ear.

Laurie's husband, Bill, recognized the simple beauty of the song and encouraged her to play it for a local pastor and some visiting musicians. The song eventually surfaced at Jack Hayford's Church On the Way in Van Nuys, California. Buck and Annie Herring learned the song there and included it on Annie's *Kids of the Kingdom.* But its greatest exposure was on Maranatha! Music's *Praise 4* in 1980.

Since then, Bill Klein has lost count, but he estimates that the song has since been released on sixty or seventy recordings, including a classic rock arrangement on *Petra Praise II.* Laurie's personal favorite is Phil Keaggy's instrumental on *The Wind and the Wheat.*

"I Love You, Lord" has emerged at least in half a dozen dialects, but the author particularly enjoys a pidgin English version that starts, "Me like-a You, Papa-God."

Pondering the enduring popularity of the classic, she says, "I feel like God not only gave me the song, but He kissed it. He touched it. He has kind of a 'Midas touch'; the things He touches are golden . . . and I think people recognize this. I also think that's why it's translated well into other languages and cultures—because it was His gift, and on top of that, it's been tested."

"I have heard some incredible stories about what the Lord has done in the lives of others through this song," says Klein. "I've heard stories of salvations and physical healings associated with it." She is quick, however, to pass the praise on to God, saying, "I don't feel any ownership for the song." She readily admits that God used the tune to shape her life. "He really did turn that valley of trouble into a door of hope."

One might expect to receive some counsel for aspiring songwriters from the author of these four famous lines. The question, though, generates an emphatic "No!" Laurie Klein laughs and says, "I don't feel like I know how to do it." Regarding "I Love You, Lord," she says, "It just leapt out of my mouth. I simply had my mouth open at the right time and God filled it."

Klein points out the rarity of the manner in which the song emerged. "That was sort of a one-time thing. I wish it would happen again." She laughs. "Typically, my songs are just part of my journals, and I consider them private. I considered 'I Love You, Lord' private. I just happened to sing it for my husband, and he encouraged me to sing it for someone else—and the Lord took it from there."

Decades after the writing of "I Love You, Lord," Laurie continues to pen songs to the Lord. "I can tweak words endlessly, trying to get them to say what I feel or what I think God has shown me," she says, although she admits that language comes to her much more naturally than music.

She is also more driven than ever by a thirst for intimacy with God. She says that God has placed the phrase *prepare Me a place* on her heart as a personal theme. "We're called to prepare room for Him," Laurie explains. The heart of a worshiper becomes evident as she speaks. "We must be prepared to meet Him no matter who we're talking to or what we're doing, whether we're worshiping in church or we're worshiping with all the tasks that make up our day."

That, she has come to understand, genuinely makes a "sweet, sweet sound" in God's ear.

"I have strong feelings about the last line [of the song]" she says, "because [when I wrote it] I was new enough in my walk with the Lord that I had just begun to realize that it's not just what we sing, it's what we say that can be a sweet sound. It's not just what we pray out loud, it's what we write down. It's what we show with our bodies. If God was deaf, how would He read me? What does my faith say that maybe isn't lining up with my words? All of that for me is what a sweet sound in His ear means. It's full, comprehensive."

In other words, it's love.

Lyrics reprinted by permission of the author. "I Love You, Lord" by Laurie Klein, © 1978, House of Mercy Music, P.O. Box 5213, Spokane, WA 99205. Copyright administered by Maranatha! Music.

12

I Want to Be Where You Are

DON MOEN

"What came out of my mouth really surprised me. . . . I couldn't get the melody out of my head."

T he gentle worship song emerging from Don Moen's lips was not the majestic choral anthem he was seeking to write. But it would not go away.

Moen's "I Want to Be Where You Are," with its smart, ascending chord pattern, youthful melody, and singable lyrics, has since become a favorite among congregations everywhere. Tender and memorable, the song makes a beautiful first impression, then ages gracefully.

This ballad delivers the timeless cry of a worshiping heart. It is a prayer to remain in the presence of God for both time and eternity.

> *I just want to be where You are,*
> *Dwelling daily in Your presence.*
> *I don't want to worship from afar.*
> *Draw me near to where You are.*

Written in September 1987, two years before the song was first released on Integrity Music's *Bless the Lord*, it has since appeared on numerous other recordings, including Integrity Music's 1995 *Men in Worship* with Jack Hayford. Translated into Spanish, Indonesian, and beyond, the song seems undaunted by language boundaries.

In addition to this classic, Moen is known for penning such favorites as "Worthy, You Are Worthy" and "God Will Make a Way."

An independent producer at the time of writing "I Want to Be Where You Are," he later became the executive vice president and creative director of Integrity Music. But despite his exposure to thousands of songs over the years, Moen admits to having a special place in his heart for this gift from the Lord. "I would have to say that this is one of my favorite songs," he confesses.

On the day that Moen wrote "I Want to Be Where You Are," however, he was not trying to write a simple praise and worship song. Rather, Moen was sitting alone at a piano in an empty church trying to compose an opening piece for the musical that would eventually become the award-winning "God with Us." Yet, instead of a commanding choral overture calling people into God's presence, something unexpected was making its arrival.

"What came out of my mouth really surprised me," Moen recalls, "because it was so gentle." He kept putting the piece aside, but eventually just gave in. "I couldn't get the melody out of my head."

He unveiled the song for the first time at a small church in Oklahoma. The piece was still unfinished. "I had my legal pad at the piano," he remembers. "Because I didn't have the rhymes yet, I just sang the four thoughts I had sketched for the bridge."

> *I want to be where You are*
> *Dwelling in Your presence*
> *Feasting at Your table*
> *Surrounded by Your glory.*

Moen had planned to complete those rhymes, but he never did. The song's effect upon the listeners caused him simply to leave the lyrics as they were. "This song was unique," he observes, "because I felt the Lord had let me capture, in music, a prayer and a cry on hundreds and thousands of people's hearts—people want to be in God's presence."

Since then, hundreds of people have sought out Moen to let him know how this song has given expression to the longing of their own hearts. The song continues to speak clearly today, not unlike King David's powerful prayer in Psalm 27, a prayer that impressed Don Moen when he received Christ as his Savior at the tender age of twelve.

> *One thing I ask of the LORD, this is what I seek:*
> *That I may dwell in the house of the LORD*
> *all the days of my life,*
> *To gaze upon the beauty of the LORD*
> *And to seek him in his temple.*

He underlined it in his Bible at the time. Twenty-five years later, when he wrote "I Want to Be Where You Are," the Lord reminded him that He had long ago impressed this desire upon Don's heart.

Reflecting on how "I Want to Be Where You Are" came to him, Moen points directly to the moving of the Holy Spirit. "When I attended Oral Roberts University in Tulsa," he explains, "Oral [Roberts] always used to say, 'Miracles are coming at you or going by you all the time.' Our challenge is to keep our spirit sensitive to hear what God's Spirit is saying to us. There is incredible worship going on right now around the throne of God involving angels and all the saints that have gone on before us. We need to learn to listen and be a reflector of that sound."

When asked if he believes the song and other inspired praise tunes may have been "written" in heaven, Moen responds thoughtfully. "I'm not sure. Isaiah said God's thoughts are far beyond our thoughts. Our mortal bodies cannot comprehend the wonderful sounds and melodies our loved ones are experiencing in heaven right now. Every once in a while, God lets us hear a new sound and we are able to marry it to a word from Him. I think these are the great songs.

"Obviously, these words and melodies are going to come out differently, depending on our abilities and our cultures. Unfortunately, we have to put everything into a human perspective, which greatly limits our total musical experience. [Yet] I do believe when we sing one of these powerful songs back to Him it brings Him great pleasure, and if we listen real closely we might hear the angels singing with us a song they have already heard."

Permission secured from Integrity Music for use of the preceding material. Lyrics from "I Want to Be Where You Are," Don Moen, © 1989, Integrity Music. Story drawn, in part, from "God Will Make a Way," Don Moen, © 1994, Integrity Music.

13

I Worship You, Almighty God

SONDRA CORBETT WOOD

"My heart's full of praise, because I've been forgiven of a lot."

At the tender age of five, bright-eyed Sondra Corbett was already singing on stage with her father's country music band. Six years later, eleven-year-old Sondra got saved in a little Baptist church, opening up the floodgates of her feelings for the Lord. But it was not until, as a teenager, Sondra began attending Christ for the Nations Institute in Dallas, Texas, that God bestowed upon this Kentucky native the gift that would interweave her long-held love for music and devotion to Him.

"I was just desperate for God, really," Sondra explains. "I found out there was more of God as His Holy Spirit when I was about sixteen, and just became so hungry for the Lord." Although she had joyfully witnessed her father's dramatic Pentecostal church conversion experience when she was sixteen, Sondra had not spent the majority of her childhood in a Christian home. As a result, she had much to learn about the Christian walk.

"I didn't even know anything about a quiet time or anything!" she recalls.

During her first week at summer school, Sondra learned that the Christ for the Nations Institute's traveling music ministry, Living Praise, was without a keyboard player. She quickly volunteered to fill the gap. ("My dad taught me never to be shy," she remembers, chuckling.) Although she didn't know most of the worship songs, Sondra played by ear and quickly picked up the new tunes.

In the weeks of schooling and ministry that followed, she learned how to worship God deeply, nurture her spiritual life, and happily submit herself to the discipline of daily devotions. During one such devotional time, one of the world's most widely sung praise songs was born.

"I was learning all of these new worship songs, and I would go over to the music room and have quiet time with the Lord [at the piano]. Living Praise was going to go out that next day and minister at a church. I went over to one of the rooms at the music building and started praying over that service, praying for the people that would be there, and worshiping the Lord. I could feel Him so close, and I just started singing what came out of my mouth: 'I worship you, almighty God, there is none like you . . .' with the chords and all. I felt Him right there . . . and that I was saying my heart to Him."

While the chorus came as pure inspiration, the verses required a bit of perspiration. "I took a little more time with those," Sondra laughs. "I wanted it to be centered around the throne room of God, so the verses say, 'I come into your courts with praise; I bow before your throne.' They talk about the presence of the Lord."

The song's simple, yet profound, message may well be the key to it's popularity. "I think it doesn't matter what age you are, it's so easy," says Sondra. "It's just straight heartfelt worship, straight to God—not *about* Him, but straight *to* Him. There's no way for the focus to be on anything else but Him when you're singing that song."

In the years that followed, "I Worship You, Almighty God" landed on several of Christ for the Nations Institute's worship tapes, which were at the time being distributed in more than one hundred countries. Sondra's mailbox began to fill up daily with requests for permission to sing the song. After Integrity Music expressed an interest, the song's success became virtually sealed.

Sondra's postcollege personal life would be off to a rockier start. Following graduation from Bible school, she found herself drifting away from the spiritual foundation upon which she had stood firmly at Christ for the Nations Institute. "There was some healing [from my childhood] that needed to happen. For about a two-year period, I just totally was away from church, away from everything, away from the Lord."

During this time, Sondra learned that she was going to have a child. At first, she was devastated. But she says now, "Getting pregnant was the best thing that ever happened to me at that point in my life. God used it to bring me full circle and brought me back to my home church in Kentucky and the Lord. My pastor and [church family] just loved me and restored me. And they had the biggest baby shower for me the church has ever had! That's the love that they showed to me, so my daughter's never known anything but the goodness of the Lord."

Throughout that experience and in subsequent years, God spoke to Sondra's heart, drawing her to a place of repentance, reassuring her of His love, and rekindling the fire of her love for Him. Then, one day, Sondra felt God calling her to move to Wisconsin, where she would one day marry. Today, Sondra continues to make her home in Madison where she is a devoted wife, mother, and worship leader as well as a prolific songwriter. Yet she never forgets the lessons of her past.

"The way I was raised, everything was centered around me. [Because of] all the things that have happened, I realized that it's *not* about me. It's about Jesus, and it's about other people. I think I had to go through some of those things. I *know* that it wasn't God's will for me to be pregnant and not be married." Yet, Sondra points out, her God—the God she praises, the One who is her righteousness—continued to love her and even to bless her ministry despite her failings.

"God has helped me to become faithful," Sondra says firmly. "I feel like Job. No matter what happens, I'm gonna serve the Lord now. I'm not sure that earlier in my walk with the Lord, even after

Bible school, that I could really say that and know that that's what it was gonna be like."

Yet an unshakable devotion to the Lord is now the prevailing anthem of Sondra's life. "A little nun came up to me once, and she said, 'I watched you all through the services, and I asked God, why does she praise You so vibrantly? Why does she love You so much or praise You like that?' Then I got to share with her my testimony. And she said God just showed her, 'Who's been forgiven much? The one that's been forgiven much, their heart is full of praise.'"

"And my heart's full of praise," says Sondra thankfully, "because I've been forgiven of a lot."

"I Worship You, Almighty God," Sondra Corbett Wood, © 1983, Integrity Music. Lyrics reprinted by permission of the author.

14

IN HIS TIME

DIANE BALL

> *"I was worried about those women sitting there, with no speaker for their event. I began to fret. Then I heard the words 'In His time!'"*

T iming is everything . . . or so the saying goes.

The only "timing" on Diane Ball's mind this particular Saturday morning, however, was that of her family's departure on a long-awaited, eagerly anticipated vacation to Southern California.

It was a getaway that had been well-earned. As the camp director at Springs of Living Water, a Christian conference center in Northern California, Diane had been kept in a state of perpetual motion throughout the summer of 1975. Her husband, Jay, in his position as the center's maintenance man, was even busier. In addition to the amount of regular work that needed to be done at the older facility, Jay was constantly being called in to deal with an emergency of one kind or another.

The first day of the Ball family vacation was no different. Carefully laid plans called for a 10:00 A.M. departure from the conference center. When the time arrived, Diane had everything ready to go. The van was packed to the brim. The children—Nanette, 14; Jay, 12; and twins Sean and Michael, 10—wriggled in their seats, impatient to hit the road.

Then their father got called in on an emergency . . . again. His reaction was characteristically compassionate.

"Well, I can't just go off and leave these people with a problem!" Jay said amiably.

He ambled off to tend to the emergency. Diane stewed.

"I was not as patient as I should have been," she offers in retrospect. "What a wonderful thing it is to have a husband who is giving, caring, and capable. Why couldn't I just appreciate all of that? Well, I had planned this vacation down to the minute, that's why!"

There was, in fact, little time to spare. The Balls' itinerary, which included both family fun-time and opportunities for ministry, called for Diane to speak at a ladies' luncheon in Kelseyville, ninety minutes away, beginning at noon.

But there was nothing to do but wait . . . and wait . . . and wait.

Diane drove the van down to the front of the conference center's seven-story brick hotel—a stately reminder of an era gone by, an era during which millionaires relaxed and played on the spectacular grounds, then known as Richardson Springs. When the children grew warm in the van, Diane let them get out to wait on the hotel's veranda.

"Stay close by!" she warned. "Dad should be out any second."

Her prediction, however, proved overly optimistic. By the time Jay emerged from the hotel, it was after 11:00. The family was unable to leave until a quarter past the hour—far too late for Diane to arrive in time to speak at the ladies' luncheon to which she was committed.

"I was furious!" she remembers. "I started to tell Jay exactly how I felt. He said what I knew he would say: 'Well, there was nothing I could do about it. Did you want me to leave those people with a problem like that?' I knew that he was right. But that wouldn't help us to make it on time!"

In the van, Diane sought solace from the only One who could truly provide it. "I began to look to God for some peace," she says.

"I was worried about those women sitting there, with no speaker for their event. I began to fret. Then I heard the words 'In His time!' I said them to myself over and over again. Soon, I felt the peace that can come only from God. Then I heard, 'He makes all things beautiful—in His time.' As we went on down the highway, the Lord gave me the prayer that followed . . . "

> *Lord, please show me ev'ry day,*
> *As You're teaching me Your way,*
> *That You do just what You say,*
> *In Your time.*

By the time the Balls rolled into Kelseyville, Diane's spirit was soothed. But she was still unprepared for what they would discover there. Upon their arrival, Diane was greeted by the president of the ladies' group, who promptly informed her that the luncheon Diane had grieved missing was just about to begin. As it turned out, there had been some problem that had delayed the beginning of the meeting.

"We were just in time," Diane recalls. "We even had time to freshen up before going into the lunch!"

This extraordinary demonstration of God's perfect timing would affect not only Diane's life but also the lives of the women to whom she would speak.

"That day," Diane says, "I had some fresh bread to share—about waiting on the Lord. About His perfect timing. And He had given me a new song in my heart! I shared it all with these ladies. The pianist played the tune, and they took the song with them in their hearts!"

In the intervening years, "In His Time" has become one of the best-loved of all contemporary worship tunes. Published in 1977 by Maranatha! Music, it became the title song on 1978's *Praise 4*. Since then, the song has been translated into numerous languages and is now sung all around the world—accomplishments that still amaze Diane and for which she refuses to take credit.

"I marvel because it is not my doing—it is all God's doing," she concludes, her story offering further proof that, while timing may not be everything, *God's* timing truly is perfect.

"In His Time," Diane Ball, © 1978, Maranatha! Music. Lyrics reprinted by permission of the author.

15

Lamb of God

TWILA PARIS

"It was almost like
taking dictation. . . ."

Twila Paris remembers clearly the day in December 1998, when, during an Emmanuel Project concert tour, she happened upon members of the hip-hop band God's Property discussing the authorship of a well-known song recorded by rhythm and blues/gospel artist CeCe Winans.

"I walked in," Paris recalls, "and they said, *'You* wrote "Lamb of God"? No! Get out of here! You mean CeCe Winans's "Lamb of God"?' Isn't that great? Suddenly, I was *in*. I was *all that*, all of a sudden. It's all a matter of perspective. . . ."

Paris eagerly shares her perspective on the song's true origination.

"Every once in a while, there's a song where you almost have this mystical sense of 'Man, that was gonna get written whether I wrote it or not!' I didn't feel like I wrote 'Lamb of God.' I felt like I just happened to be the one that was having my quiet time at the piano when it was the moment for that song to arrive."

While one might harbor visions of this gifted and prolific artist poised at a keyboard in a quiet, secluded music room, the piano in question was positioned in what she refers to as a bustling "cloverleaf" of activity—her parents' living room.

At the time, Paris was twenty-two years old, single, and still living at home. Drawing upon a strong spiritual legacy (three previous generations of extended family had served in full-time ministry) and rich musical heritage (her father was both a minister and an accomplished pianist), she had recorded two albums, attended the Youth with a Mission missionary training school in Arkansas, and had spent two years on staff with Youth with a Mission doing outreach work in foreign countries and serving as a combination praise and worship leader/choir director at the Youth with a Mission base. Yet it was at her childhood home that she would receive the inspiration for what would become one of the world's most recognizable praise and worship songs.

"I love music," says Paris. "I love listening and writing. I love that whole process, and I'll dink with a song and craft on it. But with 'Lamb of God,' it was almost like taking dictation. I don't want to superspiritualize it. I'm sure I gave some thought to 'what rhymes with sod?' But on another level, it was so easy.

"I remember when I finished, I really loved the song. I was like, 'Wow! Did I write that?' And the answer just came so quickly . . . 'Noooooo.'" She laughs. "We all have those moments where we look back on a finished project, and we realize we did not do that on our own. It wasn't even mostly us, you know? It's just so awesome: that experience of being allowed to create with the Creator, or that He would create through us."

This extraordinary creative process, Paris claims, can be viewed as the circle of devoted giving. She explains, "Romans 11:36 says, 'From him, through him, and to him are all things. To him be the glory forever, amen.' That's been a life Scripture for me, and I can't read it without picturing sort of a cycle. It says, everything is *from* Him. And everything is *to* Him. I interpret that as: whatever gifts and abilities any of us have, we use those in obedience in a way that glorifies the Lord. We offer those to Him. To use the specific example of a worship song, I'm having quiet time at the piano. God gives me the gift of a worship song. I offer that to the body of Christ. They then in turn offer it back to the Lord, and it completes the cycle."

Although the song was written in the early eighties, it looked for a time as though its cycle might be interrupted. When it came time to choose the songs for Paris's album *The Warrior Is a Child*, her producer stated, "I just don't think it ['Lamb of God'] fits." Paris believed in the song, however, and went to bat for it during the planning of her next album, *Kingdom Seekers*. "Lamb of God" was finally recorded in 1985, the year she married her husband, Jack Wright. Before long, the song began to appear in hymnals, and it has since become a beloved standard at worship services in nearly every nation.

"I'm always hearing stories of worship songs in some language around the world that some missionary friend will tell me they've encountered on some tiny little island. Then you just think, *Wow! Way to go, little song!* as if they had their own little personalities. I don't have kids, but I think just from what I've heard other people say that it's a similar kind of a feeling: songs are like children. You raise them, and you send them out the door. Then they kind of go have their own life that's completely independent of you."

Although Paris has received an abundance of critical acclaim and commercial success, it is moments of true ministry that she finds most gratifying. "To walk into a church on Sunday morning and they're singing 'Lamb of God,' just using it to worship God. Or maybe hearing a story of a little church in Romania singing 'Lamb of God' in Romanian. Those kinds of moments, when you realize that you were able to have a small part in something that is eternal, are so much more satisfying and fulfilling to me than a number one song or a number one album or a Dove Award. Believe it or not, we human beings actually have the capacity to get depressed the day after we win a Dove Award! Those things, they're great and they're fabulous, but they come and go. It's not the bottom line of who we're called to be and why we do what we do, and why we're created, why we're alive.

"We write about so many things. But it seems like for so many songwriters and for so many preachers the very best message is the one where we simply stop and talk about Jesus."

16

LET IT RISE

HOLLAND DAVIS

"God, if Your presence doesn't fill this place, if You don't come and visit us, this isn't going to happen. . . ."

not all public worship experiences are created equal. Some are awesome, some are awful, and most are somewhere in between. No one knows this better than veteran worship leader Holland Davis. During one of those "awful" experiences his powerful praise song "Let It Rise" was born.

Davis tells the story.

"We were invited to lead worship for Calvary Chapel Point Loma in their Wednesday night Bible study. It met in a coffee house on the beach. We put a band together, but it was a quite harrying experience. You had people walking in and out. Very distracting. The band was not together, either. We had new people we were trying out for the first time."

While Davis was frustrated by disinterest among the congregation and a lack of excellence from the musicians, what troubled him most was the missing glory of God. So he prayed.

"God," he began, "if Your presence doesn't fill this place, if You don't come and visit us, this isn't going to happen. You've got to visit us. Your glory has got to fill this place.

"And as the band is falling apart behind me," he recalls, "I'm praying: 'Let the glory of the Lord rise among us . . . let it bubble up from within us.'

"He was already there, working," Davis explains, "but we just weren't aware of His activity because we were so distracted. I started to play a little progression and turned to the band and asked them to follow me. Basically, the song just came out as it was recorded. It was a prayer for that environment."

> *Let the glory of the Lord rise among us . . .*
> *Let the songs of the Lord rise among us . . .*
> *Let the joy of the King rise among us . . .*
> *Let the praises of the King rise among us. . . .*

As the song emerged, the spiritual atmosphere of the room began to change.

"The place filled up," says Davis. "A stillness came upon the people. They stopped walking in and out, and the people who came in just stood there. For the next forty-five minutes, we were able—undistracted—to worship the Lord. The band all of a sudden clicked in, too. It was as if the Lord took each person and orchestrated the music together. And we really led worship almost spontaneously. We had two or three songs that we'd planned, but the rest were songs that the Lord gave us right at that moment.

"That's really how the song emerged," he recalls. "It was kind of an odd thing, but it was a God thing. There was a stillness, and the presence of God was thick. You didn't want to move, you just wanted to be there and soak it in."

"Let It Rise" captures a praise principle that Davis holds central: "God desires the worship of His people, and God's people gather with the desire to worship Him. The leader's task is simply to bring these two dynamics together.

"It's a respect of the individual people that have gathered to worship and not an assumption that we're far from God," he says simply. "It's coming from the place that God is near, and not far. We don't come from a place of farness but a place of nearness. We don't have to go through the courts and the outer courts and the inner courts and through the curtains into the Holy of Holies; we live in the Holy of Holies! God is with us, around us, in us."

Davis believes that the truth expressed by "Let It Rise" is one of the reasons the song has become so popular at Promise Keepers events, Harvest Crusades, and other avenues. "It really is a prayer of the individual: 'Let what's in my heart come to the surface,'" he says, "but it's also an admonition from the platform to let what's in your heart come to the surface."

Holland Davis's young years were spent in Japan where he met the Lord at age thirteen at a student Bible study. It was a day that changed his life forever.

"The leader was reading John 3:16 out of the Bible," Davis recalls, "and I heard an audible voice saying, 'Holland, I love you.' When I heard this voice, I felt something go through my body, and I started weeping.

"It was pretty much uncontrollable," he remembers, "and I pretty much interrupted his Bible study. That kind of upset him, so he started reading a little louder. Then he told me to be quiet! He didn't have any idea.

"I walked away from that meeting not really understanding what had happened, but knowing that I had met God. I said, 'If You love me this much, I'll follow You for the rest of my life.' My whole walk with God has been in God doing things and me responding to what He's done."

Moving to Southern California as a teen, Davis was influenced by the ministry of Calvary Chapel and Lonnie Frisbee. The following years involved worship leading and church planting across denominational lines. Those plants included Calvary Chapels, Vineyards, Evangelical Free, and Free Methodist churches.

Davis's praise songwriting soon began to emerge on Vineyard recordings and on Tim Coffman's independent Rolltop Records. He is probably best known as the author of "Let It Rise" and "At the Cross" and as the coauthor of "Healing Word." He is former sales manager of Maranatha! Music and A&R Director for their Worship Underground label. Davis is currently a full-time worship pastor. He, his wife Roxie, and their three children live in Laguna Hills, California.

Davis directs a challenge to worship leaders: "The job of the worship leader is not to get the people stirred up to praise the Lord, but to empower people to release what's already in their hearts. A lot of times as worship leaders, we don't even give them credit of having a relationship with God. We think they're dry and we have to fill them up. The reality is that they come full of gratitude. People come pregnant with worship. Worship is in them. The question is, do we have the skills as worship leaders to facilitate what's already happening in their hearts?

"They come," Davis says, "full to the brim."

"Let It Rise," Holland Davis, © 1997, Maranatha! Music. Lyrics reprinted by permission of the author.

17

Let the River Flow

DARRELL EVANS

"I went over to the pie station and, on a sheet of paper, began to write out, 'let the river flow. . . .'"

I t's taken nearly a decade, but Darrell Evans's "Let the River Flow" has splashed and coursed its way from Vineyard churches to youth meetings, finally cascading into the mainstream of the larger church.

The piece is a profound but simple acoustic ballad that cries for God to wash over His people with renewal. The song's images are startling: the blind are seeing, and the dead are saying, "I am born again." Yet these pictures are softened by a gentle repetition of the heartfelt prayer, "Let the river flow."

The piece succeeds on a variety of levels, but it is best understood as the poignant expression of a heart whose roots reach deep into worship. For Darrell Evans, those roots took hold at an early age. When he was twelve years old, the praise and worship segment at a Leon Patillo concert drew him to Jesus. "It was just Leon and a piano, but that night I went forward and committed my life to the Lord."

Later, experiencing worship at a Christian summer camp gave him reason to polish the few guitar chords he'd been taught in a junior high music class. "We learned all these great songs at camp. Worship was my favorite time," he says. "When I came home, I pulled the guitar out and started doing worship. I would sit in my room and play. That's how I began developing."

During those early teen years, Darrell's family lived alternately in California and Washington. As a result of his exposure to multiple congregations, Evans found himself with greater-than-average opportunities to lead worship. Young Evans was deeply affected by the Vineyard influence, both in the songs he learned and in the model of worship he pursued. From youth meetings in his home to Bible school and church planting, he says, "It was worship, worship, worship."

That worship never stopped. After a year at Oral Roberts University, Evans began leading worship in a Vineyard church in Tulsa, Oklahoma. He supported himself by waiting tables during the week.

Evans's lifestyle of worship led him to intercede for renewal and revival. Although he was in Tulsa, "the buckle of the Bible belt," he realized that most of the Christians he knew were not experiencing the intimacy with Christ that had been so important in his own life.

"I began praying," he recalls, "not for a man-made hype or manipulative thing, but for a real revival from the Lord. My prayers took the form of lyrics, but they were really just lines I would write down. I'd be praying, and I'd write, 'Let the poor man say I am rich in Him, let the lost man say I am found in Him. . . .'"

The chorus of "Let the River Flow," was actually born at the Village Inn pancake house in Tulsa. Evans describes the experience.

"I was at work, and it was a slow day at the restaurant. The manager was telling me something, and all of a sudden this melody dropped into my heart. I began humming it under my breath while she was talking. This simple chorus, the idea and the words were just there. So I interrupted her and said, 'Excuse me.' I went over to the pie station and, on a sheet of paper, began to write out, 'let the river flow, let the river flow, Holy Spirit come, move in power, let the river flow. . . .'

"I didn't fully understand what was happening. I wrote those very simple lines and sang it all day. I just kept mulling it over so I wouldn't forget it. When I went home that night, I began to go over some of the lines I had previously written in prayer. And I started matching them up."

> *Let the poor man say, "I am rich in Him."*
> *Let the lost man say, "I am found in Him."*
> *Let the river flow.*

Additional lines began to take form as Ezekiel 47 influenced him: "Where the river flows, everything will live . . . because the water from the sanctuary flows to them. . . ."

The following Sunday, Evans introduced the song to his congregation at the Tulsa Vineyard, which was then meeting in a YMCA building. "It was incredible," he recalls. "People were crying, and really crying out to the Lord in intercessory prayer. From that point on, we started doing the song."

Getting others to "do the song" was more problematic. Although "Let the River Flow" was written in October of 1991, it was not published immediately. Vineyard Music Group rejected it twice within the next two years. "They didn't like it," Evans admits, "and I decided to quit sending out tapes."

Finally, in 1995, things changed. It was then that the now late John Wimber heard the song performed at a Vineyard in Las Vegas where Evans had decided to live for a short time. As a direct result of that performance, "Let the River Flow" appeared on Jeff Peterson's portion of Vineyard's "Hallelujah, Glory" project. Meanwhile, the song had already become popular among local youth, particularly at Teen Mania events.

As the song gained popularity in renewal circles, Integrity Music's Don Moen became aware of it. Not long thereafter, Evans found himself in his own church office, a guitar in his hands, singing his songs for Don Moen himself. Evans remembers the moment Moen said, "We'd like to publish those."

Eventually, that relationship lead to the recording of "Let the River Flow," a watershed project for Integrity Music. The partnership could not have been more fitting. Evans sees his work, in many ways, as a blending of what Vineyard and Integrity Music have done.

Evans was the debut artist of Integrity Music's fledgling Vertical label with "You Are I Am." He followed that with the critically acclaimed "Freedom."

As part of his ongoing ministry, Evans seeks to remind worship leaders that their primary goal is to "minister worship to the Lord."

"It's for Him, for His pleasure. It has to start with our individual lives and developing that as a lifestyle. As we enjoy His presence, we're ministering worship to Him. Then we'll find it a lot easier to help other people experience that and coach them into it. But we can't take anybody anywhere we haven't been or aren't going."

"Let the River Flow," Darrell Evans, © 1995, Mercy/Vineyard Publishing. Lyrics reprinted with permission from the author.

18

LORD, BE GLORIFIED

BOB KILPATRICK

Kilpatrick compares those five notes to the five loaves a little boy brought the Lord. "When placed in the hands of Jesus, they fed multiplied thousands."

'T is a gift to be simple," says the old Quaker hymn. While that's true, few of us would expect a song with only five notes and seven words to span the planet. Yet, Bob Kilpatrick's simple "[In My Life,] Lord, Be Glorified" is printed in nearly every hymnal and songbook. It's in the overhead bins and slide trays at hundreds of thousands of churches.

After nearly twenty years, it continues to emerge as one of the top twenty-five most-sung worship songs. It has circled the globe and been translated into more languages than the author can track. Kilpatrick compares those five notes to the five loaves a little boy brought the Lord. "When placed in the hands of Jesus," he points out, "they fed multiplied thousands."

The example is apt. Just as that single lunch was originally meant to feed one, "Lord, Be Glorified" was intended as a personal prayer of consecration. "It has spread throughout the church worldwide," says the author, "because He blessed it, broke it, and gave it away to His people."

In 1977, Kilpatrick and his wife, Cindy, had just begun their full-time music ministry and were singing together as a duo. At the time, they weren't making much of an income from the music ministry, but, Bob says, "We were doing our best." Barry McGuire had recorded one of Kilpatrick's songs for an unreleased album, and others had expressed interest in his songwriting. Because he had been writing and performing since fourth grade, Bob was fully aware of his need for public approval. "I hoped, like all songwriters," he says, "that people would like my songs, and I wrote with that in mind, however dim."

On this particular day, however, Kilpatrick was alone in his mother-in-law's living room while the rest of the extended family watched television elsewhere in the home, and his heart was focused on a very specific audience.

"I was sitting [there with] my guitar in my hands and my Bible open on my knees," Kilpatrick says. "As I read, I prayed that the Lord would help me write a song that Cindy and I could sing privately as our song of consecration and dedication to the ministry that lay before us." "Lord, Be Glorified" began as it remains—a tender, personal statement to the Father.

"I think, in retrospect," Kilpatrick says, "that this lent a certain purity to the song. I was relaxed. I wasn't trying to impress anybody. I was free to write the simplest of melodies coupled with an equally simple prayer."

Following are those lyrics, along with the seldom-heard verses.

> *In my life, Lord, be glorified, be glorified.*
> *In my life, Lord, be glorified today.*
>
> *By my words, Lord . . .*
>
> *You are the reason—that I'm singing all day long*
> *Everyday is the season—to glorify You with a song*
>
> *(And so I'm singing) In this song, Lord, be glorified. . . .*
>
> *I can think of no other way—I'd rather spend a day*
> *Than with my sisters and brothers—all rejoicing in Your ways*
> *(And so we're singing) In Your church, Lord, be glorified. . . .*

When the song was completed, both Bob and Cindy realized that the little song was a treasure. "My wife encouraged me to sing it," Kilpatrick recalls. "I think she saw its potential before I did."

"I was not in the music business," Kilpatrick recalls. "I was not trying to write a 'hit' worship song. I didn't know about publishing, recording, or distribution. I had very little to do with the song's getting out the way it did. I [originally] wasn't going to share it with anybody! I did, though, because it was pretty obvious that it would help people express this basic prayer to the Lord."

Kilpatrick performed it privately for his friend Karen Lafferty, composer of "Seek Ye First," and for Jim Stipech, then worship leader at Calvary Chapel, Costa Mesa. Lafferty taught the song broadly in Europe while Stipech included it regularly in his praise services for two years. The song was eventually included on the *Praise Three* album from Maranatha! Music in 1978.

"Since then," Kilpatrick says, "I have sung the song behind the Iron Curtain, in the bustees of Calcutta, and in the slums of Central America. It has been recorded hundreds, perhaps thousands, of times and appeared in print on many millions of pages around the world. But it is still most fulfilling," he concludes, "when Cindy and I sing it as our prayer of consecration to the Lord."

19

LORD, I LIFT YOUR NAME ON HIGH

RICK FOUNDS

*"It suddenly struck me: God knows
the end from the beginning.
There are no surprises with Him."*

Worship leaders know that "Lord, I Lift Your Name on High" is a rare gem. The song is as effective in a small, intimate group as it is in a public praise outreach. Methodist junior high kids settle into the song as sweetly as do Baptist senior citizens, and it never seems to get tiresome.

In less than a decade, Rick Founds's little four-chord flock-rocker has become known and loved internationally. It hurdles denominational barriers effortlessly and is sung in every conceivable musical style. The song rocketed into CCLI's highest position several years ago, and, as of this writing, it remains comfortably nestled there. It's unusual to find a modern songbook without "Lord, I Lift" or an evangelical church that doesn't sing it.

More than an accessible and catchy praise song, "Lord, I Lift" accomplishes something priceless: it summarizes the whole gospel, responds with adoration, then places it on the lips of uncounted millions.

All of this is quite a feat for a guy who does research and development at a fiber optics company. Rick Founds, however, is far more than a techno-geek with a pocket protector. He's logged fifteen years in full-time ministry and has authored nearly five hundred praise songs, including "Jesus, Draw Me Close," "I Need You," and "Lord, I Love Your Grace." This father of three daughters has, in fact, been leading worship since he was a teenager.

Even so, Founds is awestruck by the impact of "Lord, I Lift Your Name," a song as at home around a campfire as in the shadow of the Washington Monument, where it was sung by a million Promise Keepers.

"It's an honor," Founds ponders. "I'm happy about it. It's what anybody would hope for."

"Lord, I Lift Your Name" was written in 1989 during Founds's morning devotion time on what he calls "a morning like any other." He admits that the situation surrounding the song's genesis was "not spectacular." Yet, notably, it was born out of a spiritual discipline that had been—and continues to be—vital to Founds's spiritual growth. Having developed the habit of playing guitar while watching television, he found it very natural to play while reading Scripture on his Macintosh computer monitor.

"I'd just reach over and grab my guitar," he recalls. "I'd plunk along with whatever I was reading that day."

During this time, Founds was working his way through a study on the attributes of God. One morning, he says, "I'd been jotting some notes down, and I began to just kind of marvel at the wonder of the love of God. It suddenly struck me: God knows the end from the beginning. There are no surprises with Him. At the foundation of the earth, He was there. He knew we would rebel and fall." It amazed Rick that God had a plan to redeem us from the very beginning.

As Founds meditated over his cyber-Bible and plucked his guitar strings, God's plan struck him as something of a cycle. He thought of the cycle of rain that comes down, waters the earth, evaporates back into the clouds, and returns. Suddenly, the now-famous chorus emerged:

> *You came from heaven to earth*
> *To show the way,*
> *From the earth to the cross,*
> *My debt to pay;*
> *From the cross to the grave,*

From the grave to the sky;
Lord, I lift Your name on high.

"Knowing the whole history of humanity, from its beginning to its end," Founds wonders, "God made the decision 'to show the way.' The response to grasping even a little bit of that knowledge can only be praise and thanksgiving and gratitude!"

Founds was a worship leader for a large church, so the song found its way easily to Maranatha! Music and was soon recorded. A then-new men's movement called Promise Keepers began to use the song at their rallies with both Anglo and Latino lyrics, helping lift the song into profound, even worldwide, prominence. Founds says that he is most touched when people tell him that his songs have given expression to the cries of their own hearts. He particularly treasures letters from believers in Croatia and Russia thanking him for his songs.

Today, the composer enjoys visiting churches and anonymously adding his voice to their versions of his song. He has found these renditions to be both enjoyable and often "unique." He warns young praise-song writers to prepare themselves for this shock.

"Every congregation has its own personality and style," he observes. "It's a lot of fun to hear things you have written done in the character of that church. I've heard 'Lord, I Lift Your Name' done in reggae, in three-quarter (almost a polka), and in a Spanish flavor. I've heard it done country. These were the musical characteristics of the praise band or predominant style [of that ministry]," all good signs, according to Founds. "That's exciting, because it means they have taken ownership of it," he reflects. It is yet another sign that worshipers worldwide have made both the song and its eternal message their own.

"Lord, I Lift Your Name on High," Rick Founds, © 1989, Maranatha! Music. Lyrics reprinted by permission of the author.

20

More Precious Than Silver

LYNN DESHAZO

*Lynn's manager placed her on
"fryer duty" at work, where she
and buckets of potatoes began
to engage in a battle of wills. . . .*

A job at McDonald's, a broken fast, and a simple act of repentance combine to set the stage for Lynn DeShazo's "More Precious Than Silver." The account, perhaps foolish by the world's standards, birthed one of the most loved praise songs of our generation and launched the songwriting career of a profoundly influential psalmist.

DeShazo had learned to play the guitar at age eleven, the same year in which she became a Christian. During her teen years, she listened closely to the radio and developed a good ear for popular music. As a freshman in college, DeShazo saw her musical and devotional life begin to blend, but her early efforts at writing praise songs were, in her words, "meager." Her entire repertoire consisted of only three songs at the end of three years, but she remembers that the early material seemed to evoke "a strong response in people."

After graduating from college in 1978, Lynn took a humble job to support her involvement with a campus ministry at Auburn University. "I did the thing that all parents hope their child will do upon graduating," she says, laughing, "I went to work for McDonald's!" It was a time for her to explore further praise and worship as part of her ministry work but also to learn spiritual disciplines, including fasting. One food-free Wednesday, her manager placed her on "fryer duty" at work, where she and buckets of potatoes began to engage in a battle of wills.

"Those fries just kept getting bigger as the day went on," she says. "I began to *meditate* on those fries." She remembers thinking, *If I could just eat one or two, I could make it through the day. . . .* After looking to the left and to the right, she helped herself.

Immediately, waves of guilt washed over her. When her shift was completed, she went to the Lord and repented. Lynn was impressed immediately with Colossians 2:3, that in Christ is "hidden all the treasures of wisdom and knowledge," and with this "for wisdom is more precious than rubies, and nothing you desire can compare with her," from Proverbs 8:11.

"In my spirit, I believe God linked those things together, and I began to worship the Lord and sing. The song just came out of my heart in worship to the Lord. I had a sense of God's presence and that He had really given me something."

> *Lord, You are*
> *More precious than silver,*
> *Lord, You are*
> *More costly than gold;*
> *Lord, You are*
> *More beautiful than diamonds,*
> *And nothing I desire compares with You.*

She took a few days to polish the chorus before sharing it with her local church. A few weeks later, she added the verse that many people have not heard:

> *And who can weigh the value*
> *Of knowing You?*
> *And who can judge the worth*
> *Of who You are?*

Lord, who can count the blessings
Of loving You?
And who can say
How great You really are?

Her worship leader liked the song immensely, and the church received it with open arms. Visitors carried the simple chorus to their home fellowships. When it arrived at Christ for the Nations Institute in Dallas, Texas, it became a favorite among students.

In 1982 and 1983, Lynn began to get regular requests for permission to use "More Precious Than Silver." She was baffled at how so many people had learned the piece. "I sure hadn't taught it to them!" she says. "It was exciting, though, to realize that all these people out there had heard this song and were ministered to by it."

If the song was already spreading like a brush fire, Integrity Music certainly breathed on the flames. In 1986, "More Precious Than Silver" appeared on their fifth recording, the popular *Glory to the King*. It has since appeared on more than a dozen Integrity Music releases and scores of independent recordings. "More Precious Than Silver" is now published in nearly every hymnal and songbook. CCLI reports it consistently among the top twenty-five most-licensed songs.

In time, DeShazo became a staff writer with Integrity Music, where she penned such classics as "Yahweh Is Holy," "Be Magnified," "Some May Trust in Chariots," "Lead Me to the Rock," and "Turn My Heart, O Lord." Worship leaders around the world associate Lynn DeShazo's name with well-crafted praise. Many people regard her works as genuine worship landmarks and place her with great hymn writers such as Fanny Crosby and Francis Havergal.

"If I've developed a niche," she says, "it's for the singable, often simple worship song. The emergence of 'the song' in my life," she says, "can be directly attributed to the work of the Holy Spirit."

In addition to her global ministry, Lynn also embraces local ministry and seeks to balance and integrate these two spheres of her life.

"I've always felt the local church was very important," she says. She continues to travel and teach, and is thankful for intercessors at home who keep track of her schedule and pray for her. The accountability of a home church, she says, keeps her "from getting a big head." She admits that people sometimes put her in a celebrity status, but she says, "Once they get to know me, they find out I'm just 'people' like them." And that seems to suit those other people just fine. "I think folks are relieved," she confesses, "to hear that 'More Precious Than Silver' was written as a result of someone blowing it!"

21

Mourning into Dancing

TOMMY WALKER

"I've probably sung it five thousand or ten thousand times, but I'll do it every day for the rest of my life if it keeps ministering to people and keeps opening doors."

Multitudes have celebrated their way to the throne of God riding the Latino groove of Tommy Walker's "Mourning into Dancing." It echoes from stadiums filled to capacity at Harvest Crusades. Compact discs are spinning and cassettes are rattling Ron Kenoly's version in hundreds of thousands of homes, while another four-hundred-plus recorded renderings of the song surface and circulate endlessly. It's even been arranged for easy piano.

If "Mourning into Dancing" is an arrow in the bull's-eye, then Tommy Walker is the skilled archer. Walker, an alumnus of Christ for the Nations, has led worship since his teen years and has been active in music evangelism since the Jesus Movement years.

It was in 1983, while he was leading worship at his brother's church in El Paso, Texas, that he discovered his true passion. "Worshiping God was all I wanted to do with my life," he says.

While working at a "terrible job" on an assembly line, Walker prayed, "God, if there's any way you can use me to bring people to Christ—to do evangelism and to worship You at the same time— that would be the most awesome thing." In that moment, he understood his calling.

"I began a quest," Walker says, "to write songs that would be very worshipful to believers while musically and spiritually interesting to nonbelievers." He formulated his philosophy of songwriting, sharpened his musical skills, and tailored his performances with these ideas in mind.

In 1991, as worship leader at Christian Assembly in Los Angeles, he was reading Psalm 30 and writing a new praise song for his congregation. It wasn't going very well. "Sometimes songs are straight from heaven, and you jot them down as quick as you can," he says. "Other times, it's more of a homework assignment." "Mourning into Dancing" fell into the homework category.

"It's not a very spiritual story," Walker says apologetically.

As he considered a God who exchanges deepest sorrows for joyful dancing, Walker remembered the "danceability" of Latin music. Years earlier, Walker had heard Psalm 30:11 set to a very sad melody. "Someday," he remembers thinking, "I'm going to write a song to that psalm that's happy and fast." Now, that time had come.

"I came up with a Latin groove, kind of a samba. I didn't think it was that great, but as we began to sing it at my church I realized, 'Hey, this is really working!'"

If not for a twist of timing, though, the song might have stayed forever within those walls. Walker and fellow player Justo Almario were hosting weekly musicians' fellowship meetings at the church. Their guest speaker one evening was bass-artist Abraham Laboriel.

Earlier that day, Laboriel had been at a recording session with Integrity Music producer Tom Brooks and had invited Brooks to come and hear him speak. "I think we were actually playing the song as Tom walked in," recalls Walker. Brooks loved "Mourning into Dancing" and wanted it for his new Integrity Music project, Ron Kenoly's *Lift Him Up*. That 1992 praise recording has since approached gold status while leaping denominational and cultural boundaries.

"I've seen this song used in every kind of circumstance, from praise parties to funerals," he says. "I think it connects because it's a song of hope and redemption and promise. The song has been a door-opener for me. People seem to recognize it wherever I go."

Is he tired of it? "I hate it!" he laughs. "I'm totally sick of it! I've probably sung it five thousand or ten thousand times, but I'll do it every day for the rest of my life if it keeps ministering to people and keeps opening doors."

Walker's life has changed since writing "Mourning into Dancing." "Maybe people think I'm a songwriter now," chuckles this father of three. But indeed, dozens of his songs have since been picked up by Integrity Music, Maranatha! Music, and solo artists such as Crystal Lewis. In addition, Walker now regularly leads worship at Promise Keeper events and Greg Laurie's Harvest Crusades.

At the Promise Keeper, 1997 Stand in the Gap in Washington, D.C., Walker stood behind his guitar and witnessed a million men roaring his chorus to "A Mighty Fortress." "As far as my eye could see, there was no end of humanity worshiping God. But to think that that many people were shouting out my chorus and I had anything to do with it." Walker pauses. "I was useless. I wasn't even singing. I was just bawling, to tell the truth. It was like heaven to see every kind of person and race worshiping God. I definitely had a glimpse of eternity."

Leadership opportunities such as these notwithstanding, Walker remains committed to his local fellowship. "There's something about staying in touch with what God's doing in the local church. And there's accountability, too. When you're there every week, you're nothing special. It keeps you humble. I've found there's something beautiful about staying 'the local church guy.'

"My songs that people sing at Promise Keepers have all been birthed the same way any other worship leader/songwriter in the world would do it. He'd just write a song out of his devotional time and teach it to his small group or his church."

In Walker's mind, that's all there is to it. "That's how it is with all my songs," he says simply. "I'm a worship leader, and I write songs for my church and, through God's favor, they end up going further."

22

Our God Reigns

LENNY SMITH

Although the song was well received locally, . . . it was rejected by every publisher who heard it.

L enny Smith's royal anthem "Our God Reigns" has been around longer than many of the believers who sing it. The 1973 composition is a prototype of the modern praise song. Three chords carry a simple melody that stretches politely over an octave, while lyrics paraphrase picturesque Isaiah 52:7. Soothing, pastoral stanzas erupt into a powerful chorus that soars majestically and proclaims, "Our God reigns!"

In the midsixties, Smith was in seminary pursuing his master's degree in both theology and English. Influenced by contemporary liturgical songs, he discovered his own gift of songwriting. Smith recalls, "Writing songs became a primary outlet for expressing emotionally God's love for me and my love for Him."

Smith began a career as a public school instructor with a true evangelical zeal, teaching the Bible as literature. He led many students to the Lord and fondly remembers walking young people to a local river for baptisms. School administrators frowned on all of this religious activity, and within three years Smith had been dismissed from three schools. As a teacher, he had become virtually unhirable.

As Dickens might have said, it was the best of times and the worst of times. "I was so excited about the Scriptures and worship," Smith remembers, "yet in my personal life I had so many problems."

To provide for a growing family, he worked as a laborer. "My career was detoured," he says, "from teaching high school to painting houses." Even painting houses was not dependable work.

Late one evening in 1973, Smith pored over Isaiah 52. He describes that study as watching a bud burst into a flower before his eyes. Overwhelmed by the truth that God understood Smith's very real needs and was in control of everything, he discovered a new peace. "Our God Reigns" was born that night in just five minutes.

> *How lovely on the mountains are the feet of Him*
> *Who brings good news, good news.*
> *Announcing peace, proclaiming news of happiness,*
> *Our God reigns, our God reigns.*

These lyrics reflect Smith's conviction that Jesus is the One of whom Isaiah speaks. Christ's beautiful feet brought Him to us, literally carrying the good news of the gospel. In and through Christ, ultimately, "Our God Reigns."

> *Meek as a lamb that's led out to the slaughter house,*
> *Dumb as a sheep before it's shearer.*
> *His life ran down upon the ground like pouring rain,*
> *That we might be born again.*

"I believe the heart of the matter is that our Father brings life out of death, victory out of defeat, character out of trials, patience out of difficulty, mighty trees from dying seeds. He says to us, 'Look, has anyone ever come to a more unjust, brutal end than this Jesus? And look at how gloriously I have dealt with Him! Come close now and remember: It's all right—I AM here."

Although the song was well received locally, it did not succeed immediately. It was rejected by every publisher who heard it. But evangelist Bob Mumford taught the song broadly in his crusades. Within a few years, "Our God Reigns" had spanned the United States and had surfaced in Europe and Australia as a single verse and a chorus. It was one of the earliest praise songs that many Christians heard at the initial stages of the praise movement.

Throughout the seventies, many churches felt a freedom to take liberties with the lyrics of praise songs. The author notes that several of them took the liberty of adding their own verses to "Our God Reigns." These additions did not always live up to the song's high standards, however. In 1978, Smith himself added four additional verses consistent with the vision and flow of the original work. The five verses trace the work of Jesus through His suffering, death, resurrection, and glorification.

After hearing "Our God Reigns" at a church in Texas, a young Evie Tournquist included the song in her 1980 Word album, *Teach Us Your Way*. Since then, Smith's song has appeared on projects and in places as diverse as *PTL* and *Scripture in Song*. Phil Driscoll, John Michael Talbot, and others have recorded it. Maranatha! Music has released instrumental versions. Most major hymnals and songbooks include the classic and chord arrangements.

Smith treasures a letter from the Vatican describing the song as one of the Pope's favorite works in English. "When the Pope is scheduled for large conferences," Smith says, "they almost always request permission to use the song in three languages." He grins and adds, "I always give them permission, of course."

"Our God Reigns" continues to grow with the times. Smith is particularly fond of Hypersonic's 1996 dance version and a bluegrass rendition from the Gospel Cannonball. "The song is a proclamation!" he says. "People who sing it slow and sad are missing the point.

"Most people who sing the song only half-believe it. The real message of the song is not just that God reigns over great events, like kingdoms rising and falling. The real message is that He reigns over the details of what we call accidents and coincidences. His permissive will is His perfect will, too . . . and it's all for good."

23

Seek Ye First

KAREN LAFFERTY

*Karen feels privileged to have
written a tune that is so widely used,
but carefully credits the words
to their true author. . . .*

Was every music store manager in Santa Ana reading from
the same script?

"No, Miss Lafferty. Thanks, but we don't need a guitar teacher.
That's right. Even with the music degree. Yes, we have your number. Thank you."

Life had been easier *before* Karen Lafferty decided to go into
full-time Christian music ministry. She had come within a pen stroke
of being crowned Miss New Mexico, finishing as first runner-up.
She'd left behind a promising future as a recording artist and quit
her lucrative job singing at a prestigious Orange County lounge.
Then, when she auditioned to be part of a Campus Crusade music
team, she didn't even make the finals. "I was crushed," she recalls.

The discouragement didn't end there. As the twenty-two-year-
old found opportunities to sing, she discovered that churches barely
paid for her gasoline. She tried to make ends meet by teaching guitar lessons but attracted only three students. Soon, her savings were
depleted and her rent was due. She wondered how to make the
installments on her car loan . . . the one for which her mother had
cosigned. And tuition for the ministry training she needed? Forget
that. Although she had won scholarship money in the Miss New

Mexico pageant, strict rules required that the funds be used at an accredited university. All attempts to get them applied to her ministry training were met with resistance by the pageant committee. "Living by faith" was beginning to look bleak at best. "You'll never have to pay my bills," she remembers assuring her mother. "God has called me and He'll make the way." As her bank account gradually emptied, however, Karen could not help but wonder how this would occur.

Yet, even then, God was teaching her to live by faith. And as she obediently put God's kingdom first, a defining moment of her life came to pass. As the Jesus Movement was exploding in the early seventies, its ground zero was Calvary Chapel in Costa Mesa, California. At that same time, Karen's spiritual life was being supercharged there in the midst of revival under the teaching of Pastor Chuck Smith.

"I had been on the phone all day long just trying to call music stores—anyplace—to get a job teaching guitar lessons. I knew it wasn't right that I couldn't pay my bills and was trying to figure out everything to make it work." In spite of her frustrations over money, she determined to go to church that night. "I had learned," she explains, "you don't run *from* God, you run *to* Him. That evening we studied from Matthew 6, about how God takes care of the birds of the air, and there was that verse, 'Seek ye first the kingdom of God and His righteousness, and all these things shall be added unto you.' And it hit me. I said, 'That's it!' I just needed to keep seeking His kingdom and His purposes, and He had promised to provide the things I needed. I went back home, and my rent still wasn't paid, but the joy was back."

Accompanying the joy was a haunting melody, and she began to pluck it out on her guitar. "I was thinking about the verse and realized that the melody fit," Karen recalls. "I thought, 'Hey, this might be something!'" She sang "Seek Ye First" into a tape recorder, added the "hallelujah" descant part, and, in her words, "That was it. I went to bed and slept in peace, confident that God would do something."

Soon thereafter, she introduced "Seek Ye First" at Calvary Chapel and fondly remembers Pastor Chuck's response to the simple song. "Chuck Smith is an excellent Bible teacher but a man of few words. After I taught it, he just looked over at me and said, 'That's wonderful.' I never had him say anything like this about any of my songs. It really fit Calvary Chapel at the time."

"Seek Ye First" was included on the first Maranatha! Music praise album. "It was a very simple recording," Lafferty says of the song. "I had no idea what God was going to do with it, but I knew that God was going to meet my needs."

And He did meet those needs. Within a few days of writing the song, she received a call from the Miss New Mexico pageant committee, stating that they would allow—for the first time in the pageant's history—prize money to be used for nonaccredited schooling. Any remaining money could be used at her discretion. These funds covered the full expense of her Bible training—with enough left over to pay her rent.

She had sought first His kingdom, and then her needs were met. Other Scriptures have since been married to her melody, but the composer has specifically authorized only Matthew 6:33. "We need to encourage each other with this powerful truth," she says with intention. "We have to make our doctrine according to a first love for Jesus."

And that is a love that still sees her through each day. "I have several places in my journal called, 'Seek Ye First Revisited,'" Karen explains. "The Lord has always led me back to that verse. I am so grateful and still meditating on the truth of what it means."

She remembers one hard ministry tour in Europe, when the Lord brought her encouragement via the most unexpected of sources. Just as Karen was feeling particularly lonely, a group of nuns approached her—for no apparent reason—singing the song in French. "I was so moved," Lafferty says.

The verse has returned to her in other ways, too. As a "musicianary" (a musical missionary) with YWAM, Karen has received more than half of her support from the publishing royalties of "Seek Ye First." The song opens doors for her all over the world. "Anywhere I go, they've heard of the song. They might not know me, but they figure I must not be all bad if I wrote that song!"

Karen says she feels privileged to have written a tune that is so widely used, but she carefully credits the words to their true author: Jesus. She explains with a grin, "It's an important verse. I always say, if you have a good lyric writer, you can write a good song."

24

WE BRING
THE SACRIFICE OF PRAISE

KIRK AND DEBY DEARMAN

"Friends told us once that we're the Forrest Gump of Christian music."

I t's been only twenty years, but it seems like a million miles.

Laughing, Kirk Dearman imitates the scratchy voice of an old man and warbles, "We still bring the sacrifice of praise into the house of the Lord. . . ."

Considering his and his wife Deby's journey, that humor borders on the profound.

"Some friends told us once that we're the Forrest Gump of Christian music," Deby says.

"Our life really has been like a box of chocolates," Kirk adds. "We never know what we're going to get next!"

Kirk and Deby remember the exhilaration of being whisked from private jets to five-star hotels and singing for moneyed evangelists. They also know the sting of being homeless missionaries on a rainy night in Europe with a sick daughter. Most of the time, though, it's been somewhere in between, with them learning more of what it is to bring God a "sacrifice of praise."

Once teen sweethearts and now grandparents, the authors of "We Bring the Sacrifice of Praise" have been serving Christ shoulder to shoulder for most of their lives. Kirk and Deby's thoughts seem to intertwine; they sometimes complete each other's sentences. When she struggles to find a word, he provides it.

While over the years they've written hundreds of fine, cutting-edge worship songs, they will probably always be best known for the infectious little praise polka "Sacrifice of Praise."

Kirk wrote the chorus in 1980 in response to a Bible study. It came to him while he was driving. He calls it a "car tune."

"We started singing it at our church, and someone from Christ for the Nations Institute heard it. Before we knew it, the song was on a Christ for the Nations Institute recording that went out all over the world," Deby remembers. "It had nothing to do with a company or promoting."

"Never in our wildest dreams," adds Kirk, "would we have believed that this song would be sung around the world."

Are they tired of the piece? They thunder, in unison, a resounding "Yes!" That weariness, though, resulted in a musical facelift for the song in 1990 that included two new verses by Deby. The full version, sung by Kelly Willard, is available on Integrity Music's 1998 *Women of Worship*.

Between the time that Kirk wrote the simple chorus and when Deby added the verses, the song's meaning had grown—for them—exponentially. "When Kirk wrote it," Deby explains, "we thought a sacrifice of praise meant praising the Lord when you stub your toe."

"Over the years," Kirk continues, "we've learned that worship involves a true sacrifice. It costs us something very precious. The cost can come in many different ways, but worship is costly. It costs our lives. It costs everything we have."

In the late seventies and early eighties, Kirk and Deby were involved with high-visibility ministries. They were often in the company of such people as John Michael Talbot, Kathy Lee Gifford, André Crouch, Larry Lea, Carlton Pearson, and James Robison. In addition, Deby was bringing home a thousand dollars a day as a model in Dallas. "I nicknamed her the 'Wal-Mart Queen,'" quips Kirk, because her image appeared in so many Wal-Mart advertisements.

Kirk was on staff at Shady Grove Church in Grand Prairie, Texas, where he wrote "Sacrifice of Praise," as well as such favorites as "To Thee We Ascribe Glory" and "Commune with Me."

A time of soul-searching in 1984 made clear that God was calling them to the mission field. It was a time to set aside prestige and wealth. The couple quit their jobs, sold their home, and enrolled at a Youth with a Mission school in Los Angeles.

"We went from having lots of money to being absolutely broke and nobody knew who we were," Deby summarizes. She says she changed from the Wal-Mart Queen to a Wal-Mart shopper. "We were living in the corner of a little mobile home," she recalls. "It was so poorly constructed that we could lay in bed and see the stars through the cracks in the walls!" Kirk adds, "And during the daytime, the flies came through those cracks!"

Insurance money from a car fire financed their first journey to Germany. They spent the next decade in Europe, ministering in creative arts with Chris Christensen, Graham Kendrick, and many other people. During those years, Kirk and Deby discovered an appreciation for historical Christianity. They found liturgical ideas rich and beautiful as well as useful in touching people with religious backgrounds.

Returning to America in 1991, they found the church out of touch with its own roots and have felt a call to help the American church connect with the beauty of its heritage. Songs such as "Instruments of Praise" and the Celtic prayer "Deep Peace" flow from these convictions.

"It became a passion," says Deby. "We started taking creeds, prayers of the early saints, and ancient writings and putting them to music." God has used the Dearmans to help bring renewal to liturgical churches.

Through all of the changes, offering the Lord a "Sacrifice of Praise" has remained a theme in their lives, even as they help raise a grandchild with special needs.

"It's easy to worship Him when everything's going well," Deby says.

Kirk adds, "Our worship is most precious to the Lord when we're in those places of affliction and we offer it up to Him."

"And then," continues Deby, "we get His perspective and grace to get through. It's a miracle, the little nugget that the song somehow captures. That's lifeblood to believers."

25

You Are My All in All

DENNIS JERNIGAN

"It was pretty much a spontaneous song. . . . With my left hand I'd play the piano and with my right hand, I'd write down the melody and the words."

It's no wonder that Dennis Jernigan's "You Are My All in All" is working its way into the hearts of worshipers all over the world. A congregation might learn the beguiling little song within minutes, but its haunting melody and subtle harmonies can easily make a return visit at three o'clock in the morning.

Jernigan's simple, childlike verses embrace Jesus as our strength and a treasure. The praise chorus—a true round—erupts with passion: "Jesus, Lamb of God/Worthy is Your name!"

Although Jernigan is known for dozens of fine praise songs, including "We Will Worship the Lamb of Glory" and "Great is the Lord Almighty," the CCLI charts and millions of hearts agree that "You Are My All in All" stands at the head of the pack.

To understand the birth of this song, it's important to know Dennis Jernigan the man and his remarkable testimony. In 1981, God delivered Jernigan from a lifelong struggle with homosexuality.

"He changed my whole identity," Dennis explains. "He began to do a deep work in my soul. He began teaching me who I was and what it means to be a new creation—just how much the 'old Dennis' really is dead." Following his remarkable life transformation,

Dennis married and became the father of nine children. He committed to living his life in praise to God. "How can I not," asks the psalmist, "after what He's done for me?"

"You Are My All in All" was written in 1989 while Jernigan was working at a church in Oklahoma City. "We were well on our way to really understanding more of what God wanted me to do with my life." There he led a daily prayer meeting at 6:00 A.M., leading worship from the piano. One day, while contemplating—like so many mornings before—how God had changed his life, a thought came to him. He was sitting at the piano thanking God "for the fact that He bore the punishment for my sin, paid my debt fully with the first drop of His blood." In that moment, the line came to him, "seeking You as a precious Jewel, Lord, to give up I'd be a fool."

Looking back at what that lyric meant and still means, Jernigan explains, "Jesus is worth the fight I have to go through to get to know Him. He's worth the onslaught of the enemy that tries to derail me, that tries to get me to remember what my life was like before, when that's no longer who I am. He is the source of my very existence," he continues with unaffected conviction. "The source of my life, the source of my freedom. He is the source of everything I am. He's my all in all."

The song emerged in pieces during that prayer time. Dennis would get the group praying for specific needs in the church, then return to singing. It was—and remains—Jernigan's habit always to carry a music manuscript book with him. "I believe God sings over me," he explains, referring to Zephaniah 3:17, "so I need to be listening, while I sing over Him. When I hear God, I write it down right away."

This was the process he used when writing "You Are My All in All."

You are my strength when I am weak,
You are the treasure that I seek,
You are my all in all.
Seeking You as a precious jewel,

Lord, to give up I'd be a fool,
You are my all in all. . . .

"It was pretty much a spontaneous song. I sat there, and I'd start the people praying over a specific need in the church, then I would go back to singing what I was sensing in the Lord. With my left hand I'd play the piano, and with my right hand I'd write down the melody and the words," he says. "That's how the song was born. It was so indelible in my heart, I couldn't forget it—but I did write it down right then. We started singing it the very next service in our church."

Jernigan first included the song on his independent recording, "Break My Heart, O God" in 1990. Word Music became interested when they learned he had sold or given away nearly eighty thousand copies. Ultimately, Word decided to carry most of Dennis's catalog— nearly a dozen recordings—and is publishing his newest works as well.

Over the years, a cascade of letters have flooded him from people who associate the song with their own healing, including former homosexuals and families devastated by divorce, murder, or suicide. "Especially as people learn my testimony, the words take on a whole new meaning." Each person who writes recites the same theme: When every other hope has evaporated, Jesus has become their complete strength.

He says he has since heard "You Are My All in All" in many different versions. "The most surprising was by the Insyderz, the ska version," he laughs. "That threw me for a loop! It was fun, though. My kids liked it."

His children aren't the only youngsters drawn to "You Are My All in All." "Kids love it," Jernigan admits. "It's like their song."

Countless numbers of worshipers, too, love to lift "You Are My All in All" to the Lord in praise. Worship leaders and aspiring praise songwriters also clearly resonate with the piece. What counsel would Jernigan give these men and women of God? "Seek Jesus and not a ministry," he says pointedly. "Ministry flows out of life." He remembers praying in 1985, "I will seek You, Jesus. I will seek to get to know You like the best friend I ever had, and if ministry happens, it will be a natural outflow of the life I live with You."

The result? Today, his Shepherd's Heart Music ministry is a thriving work, and his busy itinerary is not for the weak of heart. "I can't keep people away from my door," he says. "If I wasn't doing what I'm doing, I'd be counseling twenty-four hours a day. No doubt about it."